# REMEMBER WARMINSTER

Bedeguar Books

# REMEMBER WARMINSTER
## volume one

an album of memories
by
senior citizens
who lived and worked
in
WARMINSTER
during their younger days

recorded by
DANNY HOWELL

**Children at the Obelisk, about 1900.**

**Remember Warminster**
volume one

Copyright Danny Howell 1993

first published November 1993
by
Bedeguar Books
57 The Dene, Warminster, Wiltshire, BA12 9ER

Typeset by Glenn Head and Danny Howell
Design by Danny Howell
Layout by John Weallans

Print Broking
by
Articulate Studio
12a North Street, Emsworth, Hampshire

Price: £10.00

All rights reserved.
No part of this publication may be reproduced,
stored in a retrieval system or transmitted
in any form or by any means,
electronic, mechanical, optical, photocopying, recording
or otherwise without prior permission in writing from
Danny Howell.

Any copy of this book issued by the publisher as clothbound
or as a paperback is sold subject to the condition
that it shall not by way of trade or otherwise,
be lent, re-sold, hired out or otherwise circulated
without the publisher's prior consent,
in any form of binding or cover than that in which
it is published, and without a similar condition
being imposed on a subsequent purchaser.

ISBN 1 872818 06 4

# CONTENTS

| | |
|---|---|
| **Acknowledgements** | 6 |
| **Introduction** | 7 |
| **Bill Collins:** *From Butcher's Boy To Butcher* | 9 |
| **Mary Ryall:** *Like Something Out Of Dickens* | 25 |
| **Len Ingram:** *No Job And No Dole* | 43 |
| **Marjorie Yeates:** *Life With The Artindales* | 81 |
| **Roy Hampton:** *I'd Whistle As I Skipped Along* | 101 |
| **May Ede:** *Blow Your Horn* | 119 |
| **Index** | 139 |
| **Other books by Danny Howell** | 144 |

---

*"I have travelled across the sea to the Continent.
I have travelled these islands but give me Warminster,
because there is no place like Warminster."*

**Frank Moody
(1858 - 1930)**
Warminster born and bred,
businessman, councillor and magistrate

# ACKNOWLEDGEMENTS

Compilation and publication of *Remember Warminster* would not have been possible without the co-operation and assistance of a great many people, either allowing me into their homes to tape record their memories, to borrow their photographs, helping with publicity, sharing their professional expertise with regards book production, and offering encouragement along the way. I am, therefore, sincerely grateful to: Articulate Studio, Bedeguar Books, Bob Burgess, Coates and Parker, Bill Collins, Reg and Jean Curtis, Christopher Ede and family, the late May Ede, Jack Field, Fred and Sybil Gibbs, Olive Gillingham, the late Roy Hampton, the late Winifred Hampton, Glenn Head, Audrey Hitchings, Ben and Gwen Howell, the late Daisy Ingram, the late Len Ingram, Barry May, Mr and Mrs John Potter and family, Mary Ryall, Marilyn Stevens, Graham Tazewell, the late Mrs Tinnams, Warminster Dewey Museum, Warminster History Society, the staff of the *Warminster Journal*, the staff of Warminster Library, John Weallans, Joy West, Harold Yeates, and Marjorie Yeates. And last but not least, a very big thankyou to everyone who has purchased a copy of this book - I hope you enjoy reading it!

**Mrs Winifred Butcher and Olive Gillingham
serving in Ken Butcher's shop at East Street in the early 1950s.**

# INTRODUCTION

Tempus fugit - it is nearly eight years ago (February 1986) that I began tape-recording the memories of Warminster's senior citizens. Spurred on by the death of my grandmother, Norah Ball (her passing came only days after she had spent an afternoon telling me all about her Edwardian childhood), my initial motive was to glean sufficient information from people's personal reminiscences to add to the more usual lines of research (newspapers, documents, parish records, etc.) I had already undertaken for a book I had been commissioned to write.

I soon discovered that talking about the old days with those who had lived through good and bad times was a most rewarding pastime. Nostalgia? Yes, but I also realised, more importantly, that gathering real recollections had a more tangible purpose. This, to my colleagues and I at Warminster Dewey Museum, was the "flesh on the bones" of local history. These people *knew* because *they were there*. Here were first hand accounts about local people, places, and happenings. Hitherto forgotten names and faded events began to take on new meanings.

One or two brief extracts transcribed from just a few of the tapes duly appeared in the book *Yesterday's Warminster* (Barracuda Books, 1987) but the tape-recording project did not end there. I continued to call on senior citizens, with microphone and recorder, not just in Warminster but also the surrounding villages. I wanted to carry on. I wanted to hear more. Some memories were sad, some were humorous, but all were shared willingly and modestly. The result is hours and hours of people talking on tape.

Rather than merely consign the tapes to obscurity in specially provided drawers in the Dewey Museum I long expressed the wish to publish them so that everyone could share the wealth of recollections and opinions contained there-in. With this in mind I arranged 20 transcripts, ones concerning life in the surrounding villages, for my tenth book *Remember The Wylye Valley* (published in October 1989) and another selection appeared in print in *Five Connected Lives* (1990). One recording was long enough for an entire book: *With All Hopes Dashed In The Human Zoo*. Three other transcripts have been published in the *Warminster & District Archive* magazine.

The bulk of the recordings concerning Warminster have waited silently in the Dewey Museum. Whenever someone asked me, during the last couple of years, and it has been a regular question, "When are you going to do another book?" my thoughts always turned to the idea of putting into print a selection of these Warminster tapes. Until now, time and finance has prevented me from bringing this particular ambition to fruition. Recent events (including the success of the Warminster Dewey Museum Shop and an upsurge in the number of visitors and enquirers to the Museum) during the weeks prior to my writing this introduction have seemed to suggest that the time is now right for a return to local history publishing.

This book is, I hope, the first volume in a series with the collective title *Remember Warminster*. Number one contains six edited transcripts featuring Bill Collins, Mary Ryall, Len Ingram, Marjorie Yeates, Roy Hampton and May Ede, complemented with photographs both old and new. I have reproduced the words of all six tape-recordings ad verbatum, omitting all of any questions I asked, and have deliberately retained all the individual quirks of speech and anomalies of grammar, because I wanted to record not only memories but also the way people spoke. The only real changes made by myself have been to put the storylines into readable order, because the speakers, sometimes in conversation, flitted from subject to subject, occasionally repeating themselves or later elaborating on a particular period or facet of their lives.

I hope you enjoy reading the contents as much as I enjoyed listening to Bill, Mary, Len, Marjorie, Roy and May. You will notice that I took the opportunity after listening to their stories to ask them whether they had any regrets, or what changes, if any, they would make if they could live their lives again. I also asked them what they thought of today's world and current attitudes. Some readers may not agree with these opinions but I find such comments socially interesting and have, therefore, included them within the text.

Sadly, three out of the six conversationalists featured in this book have passed away since being tape-recorded: Roy Hampton (28 September 1989), Len Ingram (13 November 1991), and May Ede (9 August 1992). This book is their written testimony. I dedicate it to everyone who has contributed their stories.

Danny Howell,
Warminster Dewey Museum,
Three Horseshoes Mall,
Warminster,
Wiltshire.
November 1993.

---

The following appears in the 1928 issue of the G.W.R. Holiday Haunts:

Equi-distant (20 miles) between Bath & Salisbury. Express 2 hours from London

# WARMINSTER

## WILTS.

**A new and delightful Holiday Country, in the free and open Wiltshire Downs**

Healthful, Breezy and Bracing. 400 feet above sea-level. Situated amidst Beautiful Scenery on the edge of Salisbury Plain. Popular 18-hole Golf Course on the Downs, close to Station. Minster and Three other Churches. Good Schools. Ideal Residential Centre. Exceptionally pure Water Supply. Boating, Tennis, Bowls and Swimming provided for in the Council's New Lake Pleasure Grounds in centre of town.

Easy distance of STONEHENGE, LONGLEAT, SHEARWATER, WARDOUR CASTLE, STOURTON, WESTBURY WHITE HORSE, etc.

**For Illustrated Guide** (enclose 3d. to cover postage) **apply to:**
T. J. RUSHTON, Clerk to the Town Council

# FROM BUTCHER'S BOY TO BUTCHER
## Bill Collins
*25th April 1988*

"I was born on the 5th April 1912. So that makes me 76. I was born in Warminster, at the Furlong. The house that I was born in is extinct now; it and some others that were next to it have since been pulled down. They were where the yard is now at the Furlong; where Marshman's mill used to operate. Marshman's had the mill there, they took it over from Mr Marriage who lived at Heronslade on the Boreham Road.

"My father, Charlie Collins, came from Hill Deverill near Warminster, and his father before him was quite a respected fellow out there. Father was a carter for Marriage's, the millers, and he had a pair of white horses. Father had these greys, and another carter there, a fellow by the name of Jess Sturgess, had another pair but these were brown. About 1923, 1924 or 1925, the Wilts Agricultural Show was held on the Town Football Ground at Weymouth Street. You see, the Wiltshire Agricultural Show was held in a different town each year and this was the year it was in Warminster. The two pairs of horses were put in the show and dad's pair took first prize, and the other fellow, Sturgess, took the second prize. That was a big thing then. They were a nice pair of horses, they were groomed, and the leathers and the brasses and everything were beautifully polished.

"Father used to travel with the horses, taking flour, to Frome quite a lot. Of course, it wasn't nothing unusual for the children at the Bishopstrow end of town to run behind the horses and carts to school. Same as when the carts did go through to Frome, people did run on behind the carts to go to Frome. That's how people got about in the early 1920s.

"I didn't see a lot of my father when I was really young. He was in the Somerset Light Infantry during the First World War and afterwards he worked at Codford, at what was the R.E.s before they came to Warminster. It's now the D.O.E., and he worked for them for quite a number of years up at Oxendean.

"My mother was a woman of reasonable build and she came from Tytherington to Warminster. My parents didn't go to church but they were brought up in that respect. My parents rented the little cottage that we lived in at the Furlong. There was no water indoors; that was down in the washplace, and three cottages shared the one tap. There was an old boiler in the washplace and that had to be lit. Mother didn't have a set day for washing. If no one else was using the washplace and you could get in there, you got on and did it. Our toilet was down near the Mill. There were two toilets there for all the cottages. For toilet paper we had the *News Of The World* or something like that, cut up into sheets. If you didn't watch out you'd get all the latest betting, cricket and racing results on your backside.

"We had candles and paraffin lamps in home. We had a candle to go to bed with. I never had a bedroom of my own; I had to share. Mother did the cooking on the range. You fed it with coal and wood for your heating. We didn't do too bad when it came to getting coal because all the coal used to come by train. When they dropped it off at the Station a lot of it went down between the rails. We used to go up with a sack and scavenge for what we could find. From where we were, at the Furlong, we used to go across by the Fair Field; a lane went down through. It didn't take long to get there. We carried the sack on our back. We'd go up two or three times a week, perhaps, so we didn't do too badly for coal. Of course, there were coal merchants in Warminster, like Button's, but coal was dear then, about 11d a cwt. I say it was dear then! And we used to go up to Copheap to get firewood. We gathered what we could and we always had some wood for the fire. In those days, mother made a meal out of a few bones. She'd get some bones from the butcher, three pence worth of bones, and ask him to leave plenty of meat on. You had to make a meal out of that. We had bread and jam for tea, and that was considered quite a tea. We had a small garden at the Furlong where father used to grow artichokes and one thing and another. Father also had an allotment up Imber Road. There was all open space up Imber Road.

"I had one brother and two sisters. My younger sister, Edna, was unfortunate, because while she was playing in the Furlong one day, she knocked her heel against those railings down there. She had about 40 operations on her leg during her schooldays and she had to have a diseased bone taken out. It was one of my jobs to carry her to school on my back, piggy-back. Several of us walked to school together. I started school long before I was five; I suppose I was four or nearly four. I went to St John's School, at Boreham Road, under Miss Lander and Miss Lyons. They were very strict but they were fair and you had an education with them. I was at school with Bert Maxfield, Harry House, and Beatie Dowding; all of them. We had to toe the line at school. It was a church school and when the church anniversaries came round, such as Ascension Day, you had to go to a morning service at the Church. Afterwards you were given a bun each and then it was away home. We always looked forward to getting our buns on Ascension Day. And we used to celebrate Empire Day, all that sort of thing. When King George V came through Warminster one day we all stood out alongside the Boreham Road and did a bit of flag waving.

"I finished at St John's when I was 11, you had to, and then I went to the school in the Close. Harold Nelson Dewey was there; he was very strict, mind, but you went to school to learn, and he was there to teach you. That was his purpose. If you done anything wrong, well, you suffered. That was your look-out. We never did anything really bad, only what you call mischief. Other teachers? I think there was a Mr Edwards. Miss Trollope was down there. We had to go to North Row to do our woodwork lessons. The teacher there, Chappell, he was a so and so. If you didn't do it right, you got a piece of wood round you. Nobody would get away with it today, but things were different then. Mr Chappell used to live up Upper Marsh Road. He was a biggish fellow. There was no messing with him. We boys were not afraid of him, because we knew if we behaved ourselves it was alright. I liked woodwork. I think we enjoyed all the lessons. Of course there were times when we didn't.

"John Sims, who lived down the Marsh and was later a postman, used to work for Sharp the baker up East Street during his schooldays. Him and me, we used to go to school and book in at half past one, sit at the back, and we'd be out, perhaps, by two o'clock. Then we'd go up to a little field at Copheap Lane and collect a piebald pony of Sharp's. We'd have the pony to ride on for the afternoon. Occasionally we got caught.

"We were given our school reports to take home. The teacher gave them to you to take home for your parents. On the way home we would open them and if we didn't think much of the reports we would drop them down the nearest drain!

"The roads were dusty when I was going to school. What is a road now, Copheap Lane, was just mud. That was an unadopted road and it was nothing but mud. I used to see the cart going round sprinkling water to dampen down the dust on the roads in town. During the hot summer days they would always water the roads because of the dust. This job was also done after Fair days. They had these water tanks, horsedrawn, and they put down disinfectant on the roads where the Fair people had been. The Fair was a big occasion and it came to Warminster twice a year, every April and October. The Fair went right through the town. Maybe, you had a stall on the corner of East Street, and the Fair continued down through the town, over the hill past the Athenaeum. There would also be a bit in Weymouth Street. People out in the country saved up, naturally, to go to the Fair when it came to Warminster. That was a traditional fair then, not like a modern one today.

"I always went to the Fair, either with my family or on my own. Most of the Fair folk were a good family. Old man Jennings well looked after his men. I know because I had to serve them with meat when I was working in Archie Crease's butcher's shop. I was told to serve them with whatever they wanted. Those people were well-looked after. Some people didn't care much for the Fair people. I agree that their caravans were not as they would be now with modern sanitary arrangements but they were beautifully kept. They were like palaces. The caravans were always parked along Station Road when the Fair was in town. The Fair was wonderful in those days.

**The footpath and the railings in the Furlong, 1986.**

"The worst time for the Fair was when it was over the road here, opposite what is now Regal Court, where the Park is now. That used to be Warminster Rubbish Dump and the Fair was held there, either during the First World War years or at the end of the War. It was over there that I got a permanent reminder of it. Someone, getting off a chairplane while it was still moving, knocked me over and my eye was cut open on some rubbish. I wasn't knocked out or anything like that; it was just one of those things and I didn't take much notice of it in those days. That was a rubbish tip there, and it's certainly an improvement now with the Park.

"We never had a uniform to go to school in. You went to school in your home clothes; they were really the only clothes you had. You had to make do with the boots you wore, and your father was the boot-mender. He'd go down to Miss Francis' shop in George Street to get bits and pieces to mend the boots. You bought your bits and pieces from Miss Francis, a few nails and a few bits of leather. If you scuffed your toe-cap out then your father had to make a toe-cap. You ended up with a pair of boots made out of all different bits and pieces.

"When you were a child you had to make your own fun. When you had your summer holidays you went up over Imber Downs and spent a day up there. In those days there were raspberry canes up there and you could pick raspberries. The raspberries were picked for making jam or tarts. The raspberry canes grew wild up there; there were masses of them. You know where the Clump is; just before where you can turn off to go to Bratton; the canes were on both sides of the road there. Those on the left were on Artindale's land, and those on the right must have been on Bazley's. And if it was the time of the year for sloes and mushrooms you picked those up there.

We used to take the mushrooms to Luther Baverstock, who had a shop in East Street, and he used to take them up to the Station and send them in a tin bath on the train to Bath. Luther would give us a few coppers and we would be quite happy.

"At Christmas we always had an orange and a few nuts in our stockings. And a matchbox! Something like that. You'd be lucky if you got a chicken for your Christmas dinner then but we had a decent meal. We kids made a few decorations to put up. We made paper chains, that's all we had then. We cut up a few bits of coloured paper and stuck them together. I don't think we ever had a Christmas tree in the house. I don't think there were many Christmas trees about; that was later when that came in as one of the things to do.

"My parents told me very little when I was growing up. What you learnt was at school. I think my education was sufficient but naturally everyone learns more about the world after they leave school. It's the same today. I wasn't quite 14 when I left school. At the Close School you went through an exam to go to the Secondary School. One or two of us passed to get a place but those who failed really wanted to get out to work. That was money coming in for the family.

"In fact, I was working before I left school. I started working part time many years before. The day after I left St John's School I started going, at half past seven each day, to Chambers', the watchmaker, down where Delights toy shop is now in the Market Place. I'd go down there in the morning and stay until nine, cleaning the silver or cleaning the brasses to go on the shop fronts, and another thing I had to do was to take down the shutters. At nine o'clock I had to run from Chambers' round to the school in the Close. I had to be at school for nine o'clock.

**The view north across Weymouth Street about 1900. The field, right of centre of picture, became the Lake Pleasure Grounds in 1924.**

**Copheap, as seen from Arn Hill, in 1904.**

Charles and Mary Collins celebrating their Golden Wedding anniversary, 1958.

---

Phone 128.

# A. CREASE,
## Family Butcher.

The Best only in Goods and Attention.

The favour of your patronage is respectfully solicited.

**21, EAST STREET, WARMINSTER.**

---

Advertisement for Archie Crease, from the *Warminster & District Directory 1933*.

"At four o'clock, when I came out of school, I had to go back to Chambers' and work there again until he closed. At half past five or six o'clock he closed. Then I had to take the brasses off and close the shutters. And on Saturdays I went to work there all day. That was for half-a-crown a week and you were well-off when you got that. I can say the Chambers family were quite nice; they were proper gentlemen. Mrs Chambers was quite a lady. I had to work out the back and most of the time I was cleaning the family's boots and shoes. I had to clean all the knives and forks, the cutlery, on a pumice stone. That was their cutlery for use in home and that was cleaned every day. Mr Chambers had a lot of things for sale in the shop and there was a workshop out the back. I think a Mr Cool was working out there, watch-repairing, etc. I liked working for Mr Chambers but afterwards I got a job up at Archie Crease's, the butcher's; again this was still part time while I was at school. I heard that he wanted a lad and I went and got the job.

"I was the Saturday lad at Crease's to begin with, working on the Saturday and also evenings during the week. This was when Mr Crease had his business in where Roland John, the hairdresser, has his salon at East Street now. About 12 months or so after I started for Mr Crease, about 1927, he moved his business next door to what is now the Warminster Bookshop in East Street. Beaven's moved out of there and went further up East Street to where they are today. Crease's old shop, the one he moved out of at East Street, became a barber's shop: Ron Paynton's.

"When I left school I went to work for Mr Crease full time as the errand boy. I had to ride a carrier bicycle, and not a modern one at that. I had to cycle everywhere on it. I had to go out to Imber, twice a week, on Tuesdays and Fridays. Archie Crease had various customers at Imber including Major Whistler and the Deans who were farmers. Imber was seven miles away and you didn't have to take any notice about going up Sack Hill. I had to do this until the early 1930s when Mr Crease got a Morris van. It was one of those bull-nose things. The van did a lot of the deliveries then but I didn't drive it because I was on shop work then. I had to do a round at the Common and I also had to cycle with meat to Crockerton and through the Deverills to Maiden Bradley. That was in the late 1920s. Archie Crease had some good customers. Whitbread, the brewer, at Norton Bavant was a good customer.

"Archie Crease was a good man and he lived above the shop with his wife. He came from Clevedon and she was from Bristol. Previous to running his own business he had worked for Eastman's, the butchers, at their shop on top of Town Hall Hill [High Street]. That was during the First World War. Mr Crease was a little bit of an entertainer, with regards comic songs and that. He entertained with a partner from Sutton Veny, a fellow by the name of Tommy Hicks. They didn't do a great deal, just a little. They'd perform at the Athenaeum or maybe the Conservative Club when it was down the other side of town [Church Street]. Mr Crease was happy-go-lucky in the shop. He used to crack some very good jokes. He knew his customers; he knew who he could crack a joke with and he knew which ones to hold his tongue with. Mr Crease would, perhaps, help with the shop window display but generally we would do it ourselves. He would be there to supervise. He'd say 'Right, we'll have so and so there.'

"Crease had competition with Chinn's and also Sweetland's but he had some loyal customers. His shop was on the corner of East Street and Carson's Yard, and opposite, on the corner of Carson's

Yard and Market Place, was the London Central Meat Company. We didn't worry about them because they were only imported meats then. That was a little cheaper, yes, but it was a different kind of meat. The imported Canterbury lamb was very good. You also got some Argentine beef and that was very good too but it didn't have the flavour like the local meat. Poorer classes of people bought the imported meat because it was cheaper. You would always get some people who would rather buy the cheaper joints than the English.

"My wages, when I started first at Crease's full time, were 7s and 6d a week. That was for unlimited hours. You'd start according to how busy you were. You'd start at seven or perhaps half past seven in the morning and work until half past five or six o'clock in the evening. You worked until there were no more customers about.

"In the shop there was a counter and two blocks with surroundings to put your orders on, and marble slabs. The fitting of the shop was done by Fosters of Bath, shopfitters; and Mr Crease had a nephew down at Radstock who came up and helped with things. His name was Hockey and he was a builder and contractor. The firm still goes under the same name now, Plummer & Hockey.

"Mr Crease purchased his meat up at the Market. The cattle he bought there were walked down Station Road to East Street. We also dealt with Bernard Pickford who kept a lot of beasts on his farm at Sutton Veny. Dealing regularly with Mr Crease he knew what was wanted and he would supply us with cattle as the need arose. These were brought into Warminster, in a van, by Mr Sheppard of Sutton Veny. That was the

**The Collins' family pictured in 1958. Standing, left to right: Bill, Maud, Edna and Ivan. Seated, in front, their parents Charlie and Mary.**

father of George Sheppard who is out there now. Sheppards had a bit of a garage at Sutton Veny even back in those days. They also had a haulage business and that was later taken over by Stokes'.

"In those days there were a lot of Red Polls, which were Devon cattle. They were very popular then. Was the meat better then? The point is that it was fatter. Nine times out of ten the person wanting meat wanted it to be fat. It was not until the Second World War came that everything changed.

"Mr Crease had his slaughterhouse at Carson's Yard, up behind the shop, where Mr Fowler has got his place today. The killing was done there and this happened mostly on Sundays. That meant we were working a seven day week. The slaughterman was Arthur Knee from Pound Street. He worked freelance and he was much in demand. He had a little bit of a shop himself, at Pound Street. We used to get animals escape from the slaughterhouse. We had one steer that had come by lorry from Sutton Veny; he got out and ran back to Sutton Veny. How he knew where he had come from I shall never know but that steer got back there.

"Best rump steak was 3s 6d a pound and brisket was 6d a pound. There were others working at the shop as well as me, and on Friday nights we used to make sausages, not by motors, by hand. We'd make, perhaps, 500 pounds of sausages on a Friday night to sell in the shop on the Saturday. That was done by hand and we'd sell those for 5d a pound. We used a hand mincer. It had a nozzle on, you put the sausage skins on there and ran the stuff in. In those days we cleaned the intestines out of a pig ourselves. I've done that many a time. We used to clean those intestines for the sausage skins and we'd clean the lamb's too for the chipolata sausages.

"We had a very good trade at the shop and we supplied a good many people along the Boreham Road. We wore white coats and a blue and white apron sometimes but mostly a white apron. They always had to be clean; you dared not stick on a dirty old apron or coat. You had to have on clean clothes all the time to satisfy the clientele. Also working for Mr Crease were Walt Northeast, and George Day - he still lives at North Row I believe - and various others did come and go. Mr Northeast and Mr Day worked mostly on the rounds. You went round for orders. You'd start out at a reasonable time in the morning, get your orders, come back and cut them, and take them back out to the customers the same day. You did this locally. For Crockerton and the Deverills and places like that you delivered on Tuesdays and perhaps Saturdays, and get orders for next time while you were at it. Customers paid there and then. You took your receipt book with you. Mostly you took the money in preference to accounts. We dealt with everybody, both the gentry and the working classes. During the 1920s there were some debts but not many; you'd be surprised. Mr Crease had a very good business, it was very successful and very profitable.

"In the first place we had an ice-box to keep the meat in. The ice came by train from Bath and you had to go up to the Station to collect it. It was packed in bags with sawdust round it. I had to take some trucks up to the Station and get the ice. You knew what train it was coming in on. The ice arrived in blocks, each weighing a hundredweight. You filled the ice-box with that; there was a compartment especially for it and it lasted fairly well. It was kept shut up and you'd change it perhaps a couple of times a week. Then, one of the travellers come round one year and he sold Mr Crease some raffle tickets in the Weston Super Mare Cricket Club lottery. Mr Crease

A charabanc outing by Warminster butchers to Gough's Caves at Cheddar during the 1930s. Mr and Mrs Archie Crease, Mr and Mrs Ernest Bower, and the pigsticker George Payne are among the passengers. The charabanc was supplied by Mr Cruse.

won the first prize, £25, and with that he bought a motor to run the fridge. That did away with the ice. As the years advanced, in the 1930s, he invested in a larger fridge.

"After slaughtering, the beasts were hung in the slaughterhouse for two or three days until there was room in the fridge. As you made room in the fridge, so the meat was brought down from the slaughterhouse. As I said, in the 1930s he advanced to having a bigger fridge in another room, which meant he had two fridges then. It was a fridge where you could put quarters of beef in. You could walk in and out of it quite easily and it made for easier handling of the meat. You didn't have any of the equipment like they have today for butchering. There were no circular saws, nothing like that; and you had to put a show of meat on. If you had, say, some lambs, you had to split them right down through the middle. It was no good just banging it; you had to split it down through the backbone, right in half. And you had to do that because that was put in your window. Oh yes, it was a trade then, and Mr Crease taught me. I was under him. Naturally you had a few disasters when you first started learning, you could make a slip and that would spoil it.

"Mr Crease was very keen for me to learn the butchering. He was a good fellow to me. He taught me all there was to learn. I had to learn the slaughtering too, especially the bacon pigs because we used to do our own curing. We did the curing in the cellar. George Payne, a little chap, would come up from the Common, on his bicycle, and kill the pigs. He'd slit their throats; this was before humane killers were out. George used a very sharp knife, so sharp you dared not touch

**A scene outside Archie Crease's shop at East Street in 1928.**
**George Day Holds the steer, Bill Collins stands second from right and Walt Northeast is on the far right. The steer was reared by John Pope at Lower Barn, Horningsham.**

---

it. The bacon pigs were killed outside, in the field up behind East Street. George would go into the pen, where there would be two or three pigs and pick out the one he wanted to do first. He'd slit the pig's throat and let the pig run about until it dropped. The pig was then burnt in straw to singe the bristles off. The porker pigs were killed in the slaughterhouse and boiling water was used to scald them. The bacon was cured in salt. It was laid flat, rubbed with salt one way, turned, and rubbed with salt the other. A little pump was used to pump brine into the hams and the shoulders.

"There was nothing in the way of waste products from the butchery business. Everything was utilised. All the fats that came out of the beasts were melted down for dripping. You had a tremendous amount of dripping in those days. We did it in an old boiler. It was boiled and then put through a strainer which was the cloth off one of the Canterbury lambs. They were muslin. After straining the dripping was put in bags, a pound or half-pound. We sold a lot of that. Some people ate loads of bread and dripping. We saved the blood for black puddings. When a pig or other animal was killed we caught the blood and that had to be stirred. If you let that clot you couldn't do anything with it. If you allowed it to cool it would go solid. You stirred it to get all the bits and pieces out of it. You'd be surprised just what sediment you got out of it by stirring it. The flecks out of the pigs were rendered down for lard. Bones? People never bought bones for dogs. People bought bones for themselves to get a meal. Dogs, if they were lucky, only got bones after people had finished with them.

"A man from the Council called on

hygiene visits. The Town Surveyor was responsible for that sort of thing. They looked around your premises to see that they were up to standard. The walls in the slaughterhouse were whitewashed. Weights and Measures Inspectors called too. They came out from Trowbridge.

"I worked for Mr Crease until the outbreak of the Second World War. I served abroad during the War in the Royal Corps of Military Police. I was a N.C.O. I had put in for butchering but they said 'Right, you go to Haversford West, down Pembroke.' I got there and they said 'You're a butcher? You've come here for that!' They had to follow procedures. They didn't want butchers. They said 'No, they don't want they, we'll send you back.' That's how I came to get in the 109 Provo Company. Actually we were what they called Bluecaps then. We were held in reserve just outside Newport

**Bill Collins in a photographer's studio in Calais, 1945.**

**Frederick Gibbs**

in Wales. I finished up going through France, Belgium and Holland, to Germany. We were on traffic control for Montgomery. I didn't see much of the hostilities because we didn't go out until after the front had invaded. It was January 1946 before I got discharged.

"When you came out of the services you were supposed to go back to your old job, with your old employer. I discovered that Mr Crease had given up the shop. During the War he had been allocated the job of dishing out the meat from the slaughterhouses. That was centralised, you see. He had to see that the Warminster area had all its allocation. He was doing that job. In the meantime he had sold his shop to Robinson's of Salisbury. He went to live up Victoria Road. Later on his wife died and he went to live with his daughter at Westbury and that's where he died. Well, near enough. He was up Victoria Road until near the end. He died about the mid-1960s.

"So I came back to Robinson's. It was all straight and above board. You had to let them know when you were coming back and I did. Robinson's of Salisbury had sent a manager up to see to the shop. I didn't know the fellow who was there but he turned out to be the father of Fred Gibbs who has got the haulage business at Boreham Road today. That's how the Gibbs family moved from Salisbury to Warminster. I had to work under Fred Gibbs' father, Frederick Gibbs, and I did this for a while. I got on very well with Mr Gibbs. He was a nice fellow to work with and we had some good times together.

"I also worked part time at Lewis' butcher's shop, further up, on the other side, the north side, of East Street. You see, old Tommy Lewis had died and his son-in-law, John Withers, had took that over. John didn't know a lot about the butchery business. He was a tall, thin chap, he wasn't a Warminster man, and he was a bouncy sort of a fellow. After I finished my day's work for Mr Gibbs I went to work for John in the evenings. Very often I would be there until 11 or 12 o'clock at night, making sausages and doing other things. That gradually developed and the opportunity arose to purchase the business. John Withers couldn't settle down in business and he decided to get out. My brother was working at Dent's, the gloving firm, and we decided to take on the shop. John Withers sold the business to us and went off to Chitterne to run the bus service. He wasn't cut out to be a butcher. This was in the 1950s that my brother and I took that over. We had to buy the business. It cost £3,000 and that was a lot of money then. We took the money up. We was very good at the bank and we got a loan from them. On top of that, we got a loan from Roy Dunstan. My brother knew Roy through football at Highbury Football Club. Most of the money came from the bank. We formed a company, calling ourselves T.W. Lewis (Warminster) Ltd. Later, my brother decided to buy a business of his own, which he did, in Bournemouth. I bought out his share of the business in Warminster and eventually owned the shop at East Street on my own. I became sole owner in 1960.

"My business never failed. It did very well. We changed it into a family butcher's as well as a pork butcher's. A lot of the old customers from Mr Crease's came to me. In business, trade depends on how you approach your customers but I never had no problems like that. There was quite a bit of competition in the town but I had a good trade at East Street. The Black Watch was one of the first battalions to come to the School Of Infantry in the 1960s. I was fortunate to be able to serve the Colonel's wife. She and her husband were nice people and through them I got to serve the captains and their wives. I was always very jovial to them and other recommendations followed. The Colonel and his wife told people 'If you want quality meat, and a laugh and a joke, you've got to go to Mr Collins.'

"I got my meat, mostly, from the Bath Wholesale Meat Company. I didn't do any slaughtering then. I also got meat from the FMC at Salisbury. Running the shop was hard work. You had to hump these quarters of beef about and they had to be cut up. We made quite a lot of sausages but we had a fairly modern machine for that. When my brother and I started together we kept on the old fellow, Mr Murray from Horningsham, who had been on for Lewis' for years. Mr Murray stayed on for us until he retired. We kept the staff to a minimum. Mrs Tinnams was working for Clark's, the shoe people, and she came to help. She used to do all the cutting of the bacon. Bacon isn't cured the same today; it's all this 'E' business now. When it was coming up to holiday times and Christmas we used to work nearly all night. We had

**Bill Collins, with his daughter Ann, shortly before retiring from the shop at East Street, in 1968.**

**Bill Collins and Ivy Tinnams, on holiday, Christmas 1986.**

a very good friend, Fred Scott, who was the landlord of the Masons Arms on the opposite side of East Street. He would see us working in the shop until, maybe, 12 o'clock at night, and he'd bring a glass of beer over on a tray. Fred would say 'I expect you could do with a drink now.'

"I had to give up the business in the finish, in 1968, because I had ulcers in my legs and I had to go to hospital. We used to smoke our own bacon and one year, February time, the sharp frosts got under the ricks and lifted them. The door to the smoke room was made of iron and it weighed anything between half a ton and a ton; the best part of it. It was a solid door and I went to shut it, forgetting to take my finger out of the way as it closed. The top of my finger was taken right off. I had to go down the Hospital. I took the end of my finger with me. Dr Falk said 'Have you got the bits and pieces there, Mr Collins?' I said 'Yes, look, it's here wrapped up.' He said 'Oh alright, let's see what we can do with it.' He was the only doctor there that would do that, otherwise I would have had to have gone to Odstock Hospital with it. Dr Falk sewed it back on for me, he was very good. You can see where it was sewn back on. Some of the feeling came back but it's still a bit numb. Anyhow, I had to go down to the Hospital everyday and get it dressed. They took great care of it.

"I sold the business to Frank Whitmarsh. He bought it for his son-in-law, Mr Robbins, who has got a butcher's shop in the Market Place today. Frank used to have his own butcher's shop down at the High Street. If I had my time again I don't think I should want to change anything but I don't think I'd enjoy butchering the way it is today. Well, it's not butchering today. I mean, a carpenter can do what they do today. I don't suppose there are many butchers today who have seen the insides of an animal. They see it when it comes in four quarters, that's all.

"If you think it would be useless to even consider running an old traditional butcher's shop these days, then think again. You can compete with the supermarkets and all their pre-packed stuff, easy today. You're alright if you can sell quality meat and give personal service. People definitely want personal service. I agree that there's quite a number of people, the younger generation, who have never known what it is to pick the joints on the slab. Now it's pre-packed, they look at it, they think that's nice, they pick it up, they pay for it and take it home. But you would still get a percentage who would want their meat like it was in the old days. A person I used to serve, said to me not so long ago 'I've actually found someone I can go to where you left off.' She had found somebody in town where she could get the meat she wanted. See, there's still those types of people.

"Warminster is now a much improved town but when it was a market town you saw life everywhere. It was nothing to see a flock of a hundred sheep walked through the town centre. Or even 20 or 30 cows on the road. Now it's cars and lorries. I let Jack Field, of the History Society, have a photograph and I expect you've seen it; it's of an animal outside Crease's shop in East Street, with the men stood round. That was a Scotch beast from Mr John Pope's at Lower Barn, Horningsham. That was in 1928. George Day and Walt Northeast are on that photo. You don't see an animal like that stood outside a shop in Warminster today.

"Warminster was much smaller with regards the population. It was very reserved, you could say, and it was once divided between an upper and a lower class. The Boreham Road was upper class and the Common and the west side of town was a different class of person.

And the shopkeepers were in between. I spent most of my days at East Street; I started work there in 1925, and I closed my business in East Street in September 1968. You could say I've seen all the comings and goings at East Street. There was Tom Bellew, the hairdresser, and you'd go into him and he'd start to give you a haircut. Next thing you knew, someone had come in with a puncture in the tyre of their bike, and Tom would leave off and mend it for them. Then he'd come back with nice clean hands! They weren't clean - hair cream or bicycle oil, nobody knew! I've had many a haircut in there for two pence. That was old money, of course. Tom was quite a character. Then there was the two Fitz's, father and son, who had the blacksmith's forge in Button's Yard. The son broke away and started his own forge in the Furlong, near to the house where I was born. Button's did a lot of furniture removal and haulage, and I used to see Harry Ball and his brother, Percy, with Button's horses. That was their job. Old man Sharp was the baker, over the road, and there was Jimmy White, another baker, up the top by the Rose & Crown. Bush & Co's shop is gone now, demolished; that was Stiles' then but prior to that it was a toy shop called Faulkner's. George Sheppard had his business in East Street too; he was an umbrella repairer. He was a cripple and his legs were bent under his lap. Then there was old Mr Mundy with his faggots and peas. And Mills, the boot man. Holman & Byfield had a glove factory up the Arcade. Tommy Lewis had a room up there for curing his pigmeat. Then he lost a lot of money in the Hatchery Case thing, he had money invested, he speculated and lost it, and that's when he gave up that room. There was Phyllis Hinton, she's dead now, had the milk bar, the Dairy. Town side of the shop where the saddler used to be is where Ken George's father had a milk bar. Edgar Whitmarsh, the decorator, had a shop up the top where Bailey's is now.

"They say about the good old days; I suppose they were good to a certain extent, but you had to make the most of everything for yourself then. We know you didn't have the money and that but you had to make your own enjoyment. Money doesn't come into that. There was nothing of muggings and robberies, and you could go out and leave your door open. You dare not do that now. There isn't the discipline in the schools now, to what there was. You had discipline in the schools, and after the Second World War, when you were called up, there was National Service. You had that discipline all the time and there was no harm in that. It was after that when things started to go wrong. You don't see people dressed up now on a Sunday but you used to. If a woman had a daughter she saw to it that her daughter had a nice dress to go out in on a Sunday. That's gone, now it's jeans like every other day of the week.

"It's a different world now and I think it's gone too far to put things right. People are so advanced with education and different things. People live for today now, for themselves. We knew it when it was 'them and us' but we didn't resent the fact that there were people who had more than us. We were satisfied with what we had, and you had to work hard. If you didn't you found someone waiting for your job. The Workhouse was there for the person who wanted to take that route but the majority of us worked to keep our heads above water. We didn't have nothing like Supplementary Benefit. There was no family allowance; the mother didn't have nothing to come from the Government. What have we got now? Well, there's no value to money now. If you had a shilling years ago, you had something. A shilling was worth something then, but not today."

# LIKE SOMETHING OUT OF DICKENS
## Mary Ryall
*23rd November 1987*

"My name is Frances Mary Ryall. My father, John Thomas Ryall, was 44 when I was born. He was born in 1868 and his mother, whose name before she married was Jane Kerby, was a Channel Islander. She came here with her father and mother when she was quite a young girl. They came from the Channel Islands; they were jewellers over there and they came to Warminster to join their daughter, Madam De Gruchy, whose husband John had an appointment here.

"John De Gruchy was a professor of mathematics. You can see his tombstone at Christ Church. It's near the north west corner of the church. John De Gruchy came here for an appointment and his wife, of course, came with him. Her sister came too. You know Emwell Cross House at Vicarage Street? Well, the two sisters opened a ladies' boarding school there and they had pupils from all over the place. This Madam De Gruchy and her sister, like I said, lived at Emwell Cross House and they had young ladies boarding. Amongst them was Mary Smith and she became Mrs Tisseman who is Alan Pickford's grandmother. She used to come up Rehobath. May Tisseman, who was a neighbour of ours and knew my father very well, said her aunt, Miss Smith, lived at Torwood on the Boreham Road and, of course, Madam De Gruchy and Miss Smith then became very close to each other.

"My father's mother, Jane Ryall (formerly Kerby), is buried in the De Gruchy grave at Christ Church. Strangely enough, and I found this out from Miss Alice Beaven, the old Kerbys are buried in the Non-Conformist Cemetery at Boreham Road. I expect a lot of Channel Islanders were Non-Conformists. I think the grave is marked by one of those cast-iron markers. I think that's right. I went to the Museum in Jersey and a clock made by Kerby stands in the vestibule there. These Kerbys were in Royal Square in Jersey. I've got an idea that the place where they had their clock-making business is now a bank. The Kerbys had numerous children. One went to New Zealand, another to America, and I still correspond with one of the descendants in America.

"When I was in Jersey I got the idea that Madam De Gruchy and her husband were the children of the two partners in this jewellery and clock-making business. Some way or another he came over to England with a teaching appointment of some sort. That's how they came. Well, the old people lived opposite Emwell Cross House. I visualise that it's the one that looks a bit old, Georgian, that one in the row of houses; that's where they lived. The old man Kerby died when my father was nine years old. My father had a very vivid memory of him. Strangely enough, I sent a miniature to a relation in America of my grandfather sitting with his arm round a child who had a white frock on and a Victorian dolly in her hand - well, my dear soul, you'd think that man was my father in fancy dress.

"My grandmother came over as a young girl and she married a farmer. That was Thomas Ryall. She would have come to England in the 1850s but Madam De Gruchy was here before that. My grandfather was a bluecoat boy. He was educated by the bluecoats. He was not really an orphan; this is what I have surmised - he was brought up by an aunt because when he was born he cost his mother her life. It's just like you read in books. I often think that my family history and the stories I've heard is like something out of Charles Dickens. Don't you agree? I've got an idea that dad's family lived at one time up on the Victoria Road, up there somewhere, and I've got an idea that at one stage he was a nurseryman or something like that. I know very little about him.

"My father's father must have come back here and he had a haulage business and he was in farming, that kind of thing, and in due course, long ago, he got on the Longleat Estate. This is all what I've been told. Grandfather had Ludlow Farm, off Bradley Road, Warminster. He rented it from the Longleat Estate.

"Dad told me that when he was about 12 his father's health was bad. The Parish used to order coal from Radstock for the Workhouse and the poor of Warminster. Nine of grandfather's drays, on contract to the Parish, had to go down to Radstock but grandfather was too ill to go. Dad begged his father to let him go to Radstock. Dad was allowed. He said they went to Frome and out that way. There was a spare horse tied to the back of the drays. They had more than two horses for each cart because of the hills and they carried big iron things, chucks, to stop the wheels when they needed. They used to have to beat the horses at one or two places, where exactly I don't know, to get them up the hills.

"The trip to Radstock and back took two days. Under the drays there usually was a dog trotting along. The dog would go off and come back with a rabbit. Can you just imagine this? It's just like you read in a book. Dad broke the journey by stopping at an inn. It was pitch dark. Father told me when he opened the door of the pub and went in he saw a big pot, like a big kettle over the fire. That was kept on all night long. (Apparently, in his

**Mr Kerby.**

house it was just the same, they kept the water on because of the cattle, they always had boiling water ready for calving and emergencies). Anyhow, in this pub, he said that down in the hearth was a bundle of rags and the bundle stirred - it was an old tramp led down. People were tough in those days. Well, most of the people who worked for grandfather and father came from Warminster Common. I don't have to tell you what that was like years ago. The people there were what you might call a tough bunch.

"One of grandfather's regular haulage contracts was to deliver tallow candles for a man named Cusse. That was Peter Samuel Cusse who was a candle maker, wholesaler and retailer. His shop and premises were on the corner of Market Place and North Row, Warminster. The property was later the Co-op, then Pleasures toy shop, but it's now an opticians and clothing shop. Cusse did a big wholesale trade, supplying other shops for miles around. On one occasion grandfather was supposed to deliver a wagon load of Cusse's candles to Shaftesbury. It was winter time and there was snow on the ground. You can just imagine what sort of journey that was, going up and down the hills between Warminster and Shaftesbury. Plus the steep climb itself into Shaftesbury. Grandfather was ill and my father persuaded him to let him make the delivery. Father was only a lad, he was no more than 14 years old. Grandfather agreed on condition that one of the men went with him. That was Johnny Curtis. There was trouble with one of the shafts of the cart on the way to Shaftesbury. Father kept saying 'Get thee down Johnny, and see he to the shaft.'

"It must have been a terrible journey. When they got to Shaftesbury it was dark and father suggested to Johnny that they stop and go into an inn for a warm by the fire and something to eat. They were tired and the horses could probably have done with a rest too. Father and Johnny went into a pub. They were black and dirty and they must have looked a sight. The woman at the inn said to them 'What can I do for you, sirs.' Father, and remember he was only about 14, said 'My man and I would like some food and a bed for the night.' The woman agreed to his request. Then she said 'Where have you come from?' Father promptly replied in a loud voice 'Warminster Common.' He put the fear of God into the woman and everyone in the inn. Warminster Common had a reputation for all sorts of bad things - murders, badger baiting, cruel sports. Most people steered well clear of Warminster Common and anyone who lived there. The filthy state of Warminster Common was known all over the country, for miles around.

"Grandfather had heart trouble and he died when my dad was barely 16. The family were living at South Street, in the house where Butler Oils had their offices until a couple of years ago. There used to be a period house there. I think they rented it from one of the colleges like Cambridge. Grandmother was left a widow and I think she had two other children as well as my father. In those days a death like that to a Victorian family was a serious matter. Grandfather's family, the old ladies, called my father. It was all very severe. They said to him 'Can you continue?' My father told me that he stood there and thought how stupid they were. But you had to show great respect in those days. 'Can you continue?' they asked. He said 'Oh yes.' they said 'Very well, that's alright.'

"Before long, my father, being the man he was, blossomed out and his business prospered. He had farmland he rented and Ludlow Farm came to him when he was still a bachelor. He was living up there for about five years as a bachelor. He had land to begin with and then he started contracting. There were all solid families around here then. There was Colonel Burton at Portway House, there was Artindale at East House, and Dr Beaven at Boreham, to name but a few. All these various people had fields and horses, and my father would do the work for them, making the hay, and all that kind of thing. They hadn't the facilities. My father had a terrific amount of agricultural equipment. He also contracted to the Councils. I can remember when he contracted to Shaftesbury and Warminster Councils. That was all haulage.

"My father was a man who was completely alive. To the day he was 88 he had wonderful faculties. That's when he died, in 1956. He drove until he was 87. He drove everything. He had steam lorries, Fodens, Garretts, Scammells.

**Family and friends - standing, at the back, Miss Norah Lee and Mrs Harrington; and seated, left to right, John Thomas Ryall, Mrs Peter Stockley, Mary Ryall, Peter Stockley, and Mrs Frances Ryall. Spot, the dog, in the foreground.**

Windy Haines' father drove for us. I believe that Windy himself drove for us as a youth before he went off on his football career to Portsmouth. That was Wyndham Haines - the 'Farmer's Boy.' Dad was very sure. He had contracts and he worked like one of the men. If there were a few more like him about today there'd be no strikes. Father moved up to Ludlow Farm and lived there as a bachelor. The old ladies stayed at South Street. Father's men would arrive at the farm and knock him up in the morning about five o'clock. He'd put the bacon on and they'd have a fry up. His men adored him. They all knew dad well.

"Dad had a timber sawmill, which he owned, up where the Princecroft housing estate is now. An old man told me not very long ago that up where the Council houses are at Princecroft there was still the foundations of one of the traction engines in a garden. After all those years! Have a look one day and see if you can find it. That was all fields up there. It's all so different now. We had three mares there which dropped a foal each year. There were about 22 running colts. And the cattle were brought down there too. Because Haygrove Farm belonged to us at the time. Dad had fields from Princecroft right across to Bugley Barton.

"How many horses do you think my father had stabled at Ludlow Farm? 32! I've said to people before 'What were 32 horses in those days?' We were a triviality compared to some of the great concerns. It was nothing really, it was just an ordinary timber business. And haulage, remember. He had council work both here and at Shaftesbury. When you take it all in it's not much. But it was good for one man. You had to have quite a number of horses to take the timber about, and we had four steam engines on the roads. Those wagons were colossal.

"He had timber contracts in Dorset. Stalbridge Park was one place where he cut a lot of timber. Dad's men used to live there in caravans. I asked my father one day how many men were working for him, he said 70 off and on. In a business like that there was so much to be done. They were very well paid. There was Mr Pearce who lived out on the Boreham Road, he's dead now, he's been dead a few years now, but he lived in the cottages down by Boreham. He said to me 'I can remember when one of your father's gangs were in the woods out Shearwater during the First World War.' I said 'Oh yes.' He said 'We worked like mad there.' My father, being the man he was, paid his men well for that too. That's how he got the work out of those men. It was hard work. It was colossally hard.

"My father had a wonderful mathematical brain. Quite natural. There was something he always laughed about. When the First World War started, they felled a lot of trees out in Longleat Woods, they'd never done it for themselves before, and father got the contracts for some of the trees. Inspectors had to come in for the Government. This man came and I suppose he thought my father was just a country yokel. My father went with him to estimate the measurement of the trees. The inspector said 'Oh, that will be so and so.' My father said 'No that's not right, it'll be more like so.' The man said 'What do you know about it?' Anyhow when the wood was cut, it turned out that my

**Emwell Cross House at Vicarage Street, Warminster, pictured in 1974. This was the former ladies' boarding school run by the De Gruchy sisters during the last century.**

father's estimate was practically spot on. The man turned to him and said 'How the devil did you know that?' Dad said 'I just know.' The man said 'But how do you do it?' I saw how father did it. He'd pace out so much, look up at the trees, guess the heights and the girths, pace some more, and from that he could calculate the amount of timber. He knew.

"During the First World War he had contracts for the army camps. Timber had to be cut and hauled. There were Australians at Sutton Veny and other troops all about. The Australians, my god, the first time my father met them he said they were a tough bunch. You had to be tough with them.

"Things were alright until the First World War ended. What nearly broke father was the General Strike in 1926. Things had begun to deteriorate but when the Strike came, remember we're talking about 1926, not 1986 with all the planes and transport and things, three parts of our contracts all over the country could not be fulfilled. So father had to drastically cut back to a more rigid way of life. He sold up Rehobath, and the sawmills at Princecroft were sold. He had to sell them. All his personal land was sold. He went back to Ludlow Farm, renting off the Longleat Estate, and he continued farming and hauling. At that time it was beginning to be petrol and he had three lorries. He made quite a good income but not like it was before.

"When he moved back to Ludlow Farm he started almost, you could say, from scratch again. My uncle, mother's brother, Mr Stockley, who was at Ludlow, went into the timber trade. He became a manager for a Bristol firm. Father still had cattle - a milking herd and beef. Father's handling of the situation was absolutely marvellous. He got timber and haulage contracts on a smaller scale. He got small contracts all over the place. He kept on some county work. That's how he went on. He had the nerve to put himself in check. That's not like the people today, they don't retract when things get rough now. You get so used to something and you are tempted to carry on. My father was able to retract and pull through, and it was much to the amazement of Harry Dufosee and all his other friends. How he did it was absolutely marvellous.

"Father's tributes to my mother were wonderful. He used to say that when he went through that bad business patch in the 1920s he didn't know what he would have done without her. She was just like a rock. It's a pity you don't see much of that these days. It's a pity because that makes or mars a man. Or a woman for that matter. It takes a good woman to accept a step down.

"My mother was about five foot eight and a half and she was an attractive woman. I get my tall height not from my father's family but from my grandfather Stockley. Peter Stockley, was born on the Mottisfont Abbey Estate, Hampshire, in 1884. His father and grandfather had been the headkeepers there for 64 years. When grandfather left school he went to work for his father but in 1860 he left home and moved to Devon, where he had been engaged on an estate belonging to the Hon. Mark Rolle. He was there for four years and then he moved to the Buckenham Hall Estate, Norfolk, where he was second keeper under the headkeeper James Woodrow. The Buckenham Hall Estate belonged to Lord Ashburton, and it was famous for its bags of game. Let me read to you from this cutting I've got. It says that on 30th November 1865, soon after grandfather arrived there, the number of birds killed on that single day was 1,023 pheasants and 16 partridges. The bag also included 246 hares. The Prince of Wales [later Edward VII] spent a week shooting at Buckenham in 1866. With my

**Workers at John Ryall's saw mills.**

grandfather was a Mr Marlow, who later went on to be headkeeper for Lord Ashburton at Grange Park. When grandfather was 23 [1868], he was appointed headkeeper at Rotherfield Park in Hampshire. He had five assistants there and the master was Mr Scott.

"Grandfather Stockley was engaged as headkeeper by Lord Bath in 1879. He was engaged because the Marquis was friendly with the Prince of Wales. All the great landowners all over the country, and the Marquis of Bath was a great landowner then, had these big shoots. Lord Bath's Longleat Estate was about 30,000 acres and a sixth of this was first-rate woodland. The annual bag of pheasants was nearly 10,000. When Edward VII was Prince of Wales he visited Longleat and 1,320 pheasants were killed in one day, as well as other game. The number of pheasants bagged over four days was 3,433. The Prince was so pleased with the sport he had enjoyed that he personally congratulated grandfather. Someone else who visited Longleat for the shooting was the Duke of Edinburgh. Well, that's what it says on this cutting from the front page of *The Gamekeeper* magazine in 1900.

"Grandfather always laughed that he had the choice between a Russian Grand Duke and a Marquis. So he decided it was to be a Marquis. When he came to Longleat he was not answerable to anyone but the Marquis and the Agent. And not all that much to the Agent because the Marquis wanted the birds and it didn't matter what happened, they had to be got. I've heard my grandfather say that there were wagon loads of dates brought for the pheasants to eat.

Amazing isn't it?

"My grandfather, Peter Stockley, lived at Aucombe House in the woods and he lived there from 1879 until 1919. He was the headkeeper and he had 22 keepers under him. There was also a deerkeeper, Mr Lucas. Grandfather was his own boss really. He lived very comfortably at Aucombe House. My father used to tell him what a lucky man he was.

"I can tell you how a royal shoot went. There were all these men and the Prince coming, right? This was for the present [6th] Marquis of Bath's grandfather and he died in 1907 I think. It's best bib and tucker because the Prince is coming and everything is arranged. My father had 22 under him but the house was a great household itself - there was a coachman who was completely the boss of his department, and a head forester who was completely the boss of his department, and don't forget the gardens. Oh, a terrific staff. Forty indoor servants and all the ladies' maids and what have you. Plus tutors and all the rest of it. It was just like a battle field with this royal shoot.

"The Marquis spent a certain amount of each year in Italy, he died in Italy, but when he was at Longleat he would see each head of department one day each week. And that was at six o'clock in the evening. My grandfather's day was Tuesday. You can imagine him going down to Longleat House in his trap. He'd go into the steward's room. Mr Holmes, who retired to Mere, was the steward and he was the last steward. After that it was just butlers and what have you. Mr Holmes' father had been private coachman to Prince Edward himself.

**Rehobath Farmhouse, about 1920.**

My grandfather would interview the men in his charge. The etiquette was colossal. I dare say it's still the same in royal circles today. The equerry loaded for his master - the Prince. The headkeeper loaded for his master - the Marquis. According to the rank of each gentleman it was done, and it was so, so, so. They had to learn how to address their masters properly and they had to be sure to heed it. There was an instance when a Russian was present who had to be called 'Highness'. The men were told. 'Oh yes, oh yes,' said one man. The men would go through it, again and again, who was to be called 'Sir' and whatever. This man kept forgetting but at last they thought he had it right. The time came. There was the Prince, there was the Marquis, there was the equerry, there was my grandfather, and there was this man who thought he could remember what he had to say. He got muddled. When he was presented to His Highness he said 'My lord, er sir, oh damn he, I don't know what to call he!' and of course, afterwards, my grandfather apologised to the Marquis. 'Doesn't matter Stockley' he said 'It kept the dinner table alive with conversation.' You see the Prince had roared with laughter to hear that man fumbling.

"A tent used to be put up when the shoot was on. Sometimes it was put up at the bottom of Cannimore Hollow. The ladies, including the Princess, would join in the shooting party for lunch. The footmen would bring all the stuff out. When the gentry had finished, the Marquis would beckon to grandfather and he would perhaps compliment him on the day's bag, or discuss how things went.

**The Cannimore Brook at Rehobath, about 1920.**

"My mother told me how the banqueting hall at Longleat House was a complete and utter picture. Mr Holmes used to give a reception to the heads of departments and when my mother was engaged she went down there with my father. I think King Edward VII and Alexandra were there at the time. In the Great Hall there's a peeping place where the ladies can stand and watch, and there was a little reception in the steward's room. You could look down over and my mother said it was out of this world. To see them all, the royal party and the gentry, in their finery. I think my mother saw it like that twice, on her engagement and once after she married.

"How did my father meet my mother? One of the men said to my father 'Mr Stockley, out at Aucombe, he's got a couple of Jersey cows and he wants the hay cut in a couple of meadows.' I think my father knew Mr Stockley. Father said 'Oh, I'll go out there one morning and see.' He went out and knocked Mr Stockley's door. The lady who did the housework out there, Mrs Dredge, she came to the door and said 'Mr Stockley is out somewhere.' With that, this haughty figure came along the path and said 'Yes.' That was the first time my father set eyes upon my mother!

"It didn't seem to start off too well. I suppose she thought him a nuisance coming there when her father was out. Eventually, the old man came back and said to my father 'Have you had breakfast yet?' 'No,' replied my father. Mr Stockley said 'Come on in then and have some.' My father later told me 'You never saw anything like it. There was a rabbit pie as big as Cley Hill, with bacon and all the rest of it in.' That's where my father first saw my mother but they thought nothing about each other. The Fair used to come to Warminster twice a year, in April and October. Warminster Fair was a big do. My father went to this Fair and he saw this young woman, Frances Stockley, again, in a horse and trap with her two young brothers. They were younger than her, because her father had re-married after his first wife died. Anyhow, that's how these things happen.

"Mother and father's romance began and they married at Longbridge Deverill. There was an old Miss Curtis, she's dead now, but she used to work in Mrs Butler's workroom. She was Roy Curtis' sister and she lived in King Street. She always used to laugh and tell me this, she said the windows of Mrs Butler's were wide open one morning and the bells of Longbridge Deverill were going at one o'clock. Someone in Mrs Butler's casually said 'Oh I wonder who they're for?' They were told they were for Miss Stockley's wedding. Miss Curtis was very friendly with my mother.

"Mother and father married in 1909. I think the date was 17th May. They went to London for their honeymoon. I had no idea of this until Miss Judy Foreman, Herbert Foreman's sister, told me. Her aunts were friends of my mother's. One of Judy's aunts kept the cuttings of all her friends' weddings. When the old lady died Judy said to me 'I've got the cutting of your father and mother's wedding.' She gave it to me and I've still got it.

It reads 'Longbridge Deverill - Wedding. A quiet but pretty wedding took place at the Parish church on Wednesday. The contracting parties were Mr John T. Ryall of Warminster and Miss Frances J. Stockley, daughter of Mr Peter Stockley of Aucombe, Lord Bath's headkeeper. The bride, who was attired in her travelling dress and carried a shower bouquet of white flowers, was given away by her father and was attended by Miss Nellie Cameron as bridesmaid. Mr S. Stockley acted as best men. The Vicar, the Rev R. G. Penny, officiated at the service. Many peals were rung on the bells as the happy couple left

Celia and Tizzie Chambers, with pupils at their school, about 1919.

The Great Hall at Longleat House, during the 1930s.

**St Monica's School at Vicarage Street, 1928.**

**Inside the Chapel at St Monica's School, on St Monica's Day, 1928.**

the church and were driven to Westbury Station en route to London where the honeymoon is being spent. The presents received were handsome and numerous.' May 19th 1909 is written on the back.

"My parents set up home at Ludlow Farm, off Bradley Road, Warminster. That's where I was born just before the First World War, in 1912. The doctor, who delivered me, was Dr Hubert Willcox. He died a year after I was born. My mother told me how he died of blood poisoning. My father loved the Willcoxs. They were well known here. My father always said that the death of Hubert Willcox was one of the biggest tragedies - he was a delightful man. He'd come to the outlying farms in a pony and trap. I was born about three o'clock in the morning. There were a lot of illnesses about at that time, it was March, and the doctor looked exhausted. He had been out making call after call. My father told Dr Willcox to use the spare bed. He said 'Get yourself some sleep in for a couple of hours.' He had a nap. He came again on Sunday after I was born and he told my mother 'A friend of yours has got a little girl.' That was my friend Mary Harding, Mary Pickford. She was born at Manor Farm, Longbridge Deverill. I was the last child born at Ludlow. The Rendell family had Ludlow Farm after us but their children were born in a nursing home or a maternity hospital. So, I was the last child born there. I think I'm right in saying that Peter Pickford, who is now sadly dead, was the last child born at Botany, next door to Ludlow Farm.

"Home life was very merry when I was growing up. I was an only child. Florrie Lidbury joined us when I was about three years old, she was like a nanny. She went everywhere with me until I was about 11 years old. She was a wonderful woman. Old Elsie, with the poodle, is her sister. She's the last one. Florrie is dead, she died of cancer, unfortunately. She was a Warminster person. Her family lived up at the top of Hillwood. In those days being a nanny was a nice little job for a young girl. The Pickfords had two nannies because there were seven children. Florrie was about 14 or 15 when she came to be my nanny. She went everywhere with me. She had a much better life than someone in a factory, that was rougher there.

"When I was two or three years old my family moved from Ludlow Farm to Rehobath. That's where we went to live. Father's business had expanded but he'd had Rehobath already for some years. An uncle, who was working with father, moved to Ludlow. I can remember a nanny goat that we had there. You published a photograph on page 128 of your book *Yesterday's Warminster*. It shows father and me with the goat.

"Father had bought Rehobath from the auctioneer, Mr Low. In those days the walls were flat but it's got bay windows now. The house is called Byways today. That's where I spent my childhood. There were gardens at Rehobath and they were a children's paradise. There were sand caves in the garden and there was a ruined chapel in the grounds. There was a crystal clear trout stream that came down to a little waterfall. That used to come right down between the houses and lawns and flow out under and on down the Common. My contemporaries today, Marjorie Cox and some of the older Pickfords (now no longer with us) used to have a whale of a time at the gardens in Rehobath.

"What we adored more than anything else was daring on other children, we were terrible for that. I remember there was a whole gang of us down there one day and a cousin of mine came from Bristol. We were the same age. I still laugh about this today. Florrie Lidbury was supposed to be looking after him. His mother and Florrie were clack

**A scene at Aucombe, on the Longleat Estate, about 1908.
Frances Stockley (later Mrs John Thomas Ryall) admiring one of her father's
Jersey house cows.**

clacking in the house and he rushes out. There was a whole gang of us, we were running down the slope and lawn and jumping over the stream. Of course we were very clever at that because we had done it so many times before. This little boy tries it and he landed in the middle of the stream! I can 'see' him now. He was sent up to my bedroom and put in one of my nightgowns because his clothes were wet and had to be dried. That poor little boy was sitting up in my window, crying his eyes out. He was watching us and we were all laughing like demons. You know what children are.

"I was five when I started school at Miss Chambers', up where Emlyn Rees lives now, off the south side of the Market Place. There were the two Miss Chambers, Celia and Tizzie, and they were handsome women. They were the daughters of the jeweller. Bert Chambers was their brother. Miss Celia was a beautiful woman. An aunt of mine took me in to my first day at the school. We went in by pony and trap. I remember on that first day seeing the staircase in the place, it wound a bit, and Miss Celia came down it, wearing a long white string of pearls.

"Celia and Tizzie lived until they were nearly 90. Aunty and I were waiting for somebody one day, years after I had left school, and Miss Celia came along. she said 'Do come up and see Tizzie and have a sherry.' We went up. Tizzie told us how she was going to be 90 in two years time and she wanted to have a marvellous party but of course it never happened. Eventually, Celia and Tizzie went to a ladies' home in Bristol.

"Richard Chambers, their nephew, was a pupil at the school. He died in the War, he wasn't killed by the enemy, he died of sandfly fever. I can remember a lot of my school pals. There was Grace and Geoffrey Butcher; Austen Pickford; Hugh Pickford, who was killed in the War; the two Harraway boys; Mary Hatton; Betty Joyce; and Jimmy Lidbury, who was also killed in the War. Jimmy's father had the Old Bell Hotel.

"We used to have marvellous parties. We all had very indulgent parents. Mrs Hatton used to give a whale of a party. Mrs George Pickford did the same and my mother gave another. Tom Bazley's was another affair. We'd have about ten Christmas parties every year. In those days the Victorians, like the Edwardians and early Georgians, made merry. There was more going on, these parties went on at each other's homes. They were fun but we were taught to behave; there was no scrabbling about or anything like that.

"Life at school was very happy but very strict. Those who lived out in the country boarded during the week and the others, who lived in town, went daily. We took our sandwiches for lunch. We were taught to sit down at the table and Miss Chambers would allow you to drink but you were not allowed to drink while you were eating. When you spoke to her you had to look at her straight in the face. She kept the cane on the mantelpiece. I only saw it used once. When it came to history lessons we were taught famous dates. I think I can still say my dates today as she taught us; I don't suppose there are many women in the generation younger than me who can do that.

"I went to the Chambers' School until I was about eight and then I went to St Monica's School at Vicarage Street. There again, it was happy but we were very strictly brought up. Sir James Erasmus Philipps founded the school. We were taught by the nuns from St Denys' Convent. It's not like Warminster School is today. It was all nuns back then except for a Miss Glubb and she taught English I think. She wasn't a local person and I don't know where she went in the end. The nuns were charming. Sister Ada was the headmistress. Sister Ida Mary taught Latin and she later became the headmistress. Sister Constance taught maths. Sister May looked after the moral side of our upbringing. That's how it was in those days. She conducted us, she was like a mother-figure. She was an original girl of the school. Sister May was a charming lady.

"We were well educated. There were a lot of boarders as well as day girls. In the summer we wore just ordinary top frocks but they had to be a light colour and have short sleeves. We were allowed to wear socks in the summer, white socks until we were about 12 or 14. Then we had to wear black stockings. We wore a gym slip and two kinds of blouses were allowed. The day girls wore a striped sort of band around their hats. The day girls wore a mauve shield and the boarders a blue shield. After a while it was changed.

"We had swimming lessons. Mr Huby Day (Sidney Day's father), who lived at Ash Walk, did the maintenance work at the school, and this is extraordinary, he was our tutor for swimming! My father thought it hilarious - all those nuns but they had a man to teach us to swim! Mr Day was jolly good. I don't know how he got the job. I suppose doing the maintenance work he just got roped in because he knew how to swim. We used to go along to the Park, off Weymouth Street, when the open air swimming baths there were completely new. This is long before Warminster School had their own baths. We used to go twice a week. We'd go down to Vicarage Street, along Emwell Street, then up Primrose Lane to Weymouth Street, out that way, in a crocodile. We had mademoiselle with us and a sister and Mr Day. We had to get certificates for swimming 50 yards first and then 100 yards. After that you were allowed to swim just as you liked.

"I was 16 and a half when I left St Monica's. I had a few months at home. I was told very firmly by my mother 'Now, make up your mind what you want to do.' My father said 'Oh, don't bother about that' but my mother said 'Yes we do need to bother.' Father was very easy going towards me. Mother said 'I stayed at home and if I had ten children I'd never let one of them stay at home.' She reckoned it was bad for you which is perfectly true. So I had about six months at home. It was very nice. I joined the tennis club which had just been founded at the Park. I had some great fun there.

"By the end of the summer my mother had made arrangements with Bloom's at Salisbury. That was a very exclusive dress shop. Bloom's is now Dingles. I

**Mary Ryall, beside the stream at Rehobath, 1926.**

**Mary Ryall, aged 15, with dogs Jock and Sandy.**

wanted to do fashions. I went into Bloom's. After six months probation you were then signed on. There were no wages in the probation period. The premium was round about £100. My parents paid that for my training. The firm kept us. We lived in. There was a housekeeper. We were fed, if you could call it feeding, and we lived in the house. There were five apprentices there. We were allowed out until 10 o'clock at night.

"About 1929 business everywhere was very hard to maintain and Bloom's went under. They were bought up by Guards of Wimbledon and became known as Blooms (Salisbury) Ltd. That was a tragedy. The business had been founded by Mr and Mrs Bloom. Tom Bloom became one of the directors of the new company. He had the ground floor and

Mr Layes' brother-in-law had our floor. After the six months' probation the apprenticeship papers were sent to your parents to sign. You were then called into the office and you had to sign the papers as well. These two men stood there. One said 'You sign it.' I went to sign it but he made me jump. He said 'You never sign anything without reading it.' Then he said 'I see your mother was a Stockley.' I said 'Yes.' He said 'Was her uncle's name Harry?' I said 'Yes, that's right.' He said 'Oh, I knew him well.'

"My grandfather's brother, Harry Stockley, was a big bookie at Eastleigh and he used to come through to Salisbury, where he stayed at the Red Lion, collecting his books, his bets, before moving on to Warminster to have a shoot with my grandfather. Sometimes he would go on to Wincanton Races or

**Frances Ryall and daughter Mary with dog Spot and cats Peter and Nicco.**

something like that before going back in his pony and trap to Salisbury and home. When I told my father this he said 'I expect your boss knew old Harry well.'

"It was not easy working in the shop. We had to sell fashions but we were not allowed to approach a customer until we had been there six months. The clientele was so different to what it is today. They were mostly titled and county people. After my apprenticeship they didn't keep me on. Apprentices were got shot of because the company wanted others paying them £100 for the privilege. By that time they had abandoned the living-in place, they stopped that when they became Blooms (Salisbury) Ltd. We lived out. We were farmed out on the town. Apprenticeship over, I spent two months living at home.

"Then I got with Plummer's at

**Mary with her father John Ryall.**

Southampton. From there I went to Evans & Allan at Bath. The managing director at Owens' was our buyer. The first sales left and by that time I had been brought up to a second and I managed for him. I was only about 22. For six to eight weeks Miss Fisher kept saying 'Why don't you ask him for the job?' I did. 'Oh, you're miles too young' he said. I thought 'Oh very well' but it was embarrassing. When you had been working in the shop for some time the customers start to ask for you and it was very awkward when someone else came in because the customers ignore them and walk past them to you.

"Then I saw this job going at Style & Gerrish in Salisbury, which in those days was a lovely shop. It was like Bloom's but a farmer's trade, catering for landowners and the like. It was a beautiful shop, not like it is today. Debenhams have got it now and they've ruined it. That's my opinion. I went there and got the job, working with Mrs Tevenham. She and I had eight girls in the end. We ran the gowns and coats and nightwear. Then the Second World War started. We had a manager, Mr Nelm, who had come from Harrod's in London. We worked with him for some years. We were a young staff to start with and we did well there.

"I wanted to join up but Mr Nelm wouldn't allow me. There was some rubbish about all first sales being under an umbrella but of course we were called up. I wanted to go in the Wrens but that was closed, the Air Force was closed, it was too late. There was the ATS but I didn't want to go in the ATS. Mr Nelm said 'You've got staff experience, I can get you into industry.' I said 'Fair enough, that's alright.' I went to Wellworthy's for three months. Mrs and I took 25 girls down to Lymington every day for training. Whilst they were down there we walked the floors with the inspectors. My golly, that was something, 2,000 on a shift. Gosh, that was an eye-opener I can tell you. Then we came back to Salisbury and opened up there.

"Suddenly my mother's health was deteriorating very badly. Dr Hogan said to me 'Really you should be at home.' But I had been trained for this job. It was very difficult to get out of it. Anyhow I got out. I approached the man who was in charge. He happened to come in one day and I had a word with him. He said he would understand if I went. I went before a tribunal and got out. It was because of the farm. We had land girls. This was 1942. I came back home. My mother died four and a half years afterwards. She had heart trouble and died in 1946. Her heart was very bad. Today, I know someone who had the same trouble and they're alright. Father and I came to live here, on the Boreham Road, in 1951. He died in 1956. Father and mother are buried at Christ Church. Their grave is marked. It's in the new piece and my aunt's ashes are in there too.

"Looking back, thinking of Warminster, it's sad, very sad. Sad because so much of it changing and not for the better. There's too much building going on now. For instance, Plants Green is very nice but to poke those three or four big houses [Chelwood Court] in that corner behind Ulster Lodge is ridiculous. And that's what they're doing all over the place. The Conservative Club was nice, had they put a couple of discreet bungalows there but to put those great big houses there, well, I don't think much of that. Those houses on the Boreham Road are bad enough but I hear now they're going to stick another load in behind Prestbury House [Canon's Close]. I don't like all that kind of thing. It's only done for money. And I'm heartbroken about the closure of Wilson and Kennard's shop. What is it all coming to?"

# NO JOB AND NO DOLE
## Len Ingram
*9 May 1988*

"My name is Leonard William Ingram and I was born in a small cottage at Pound Street, Warminster, which is still there. That was number 93 but the number has been altered since [now No. 10]. It's at the West Street end of Pound Street. It's on the right hand side as you go up towards the Maltings. The cottage I lived in juts out a bit, it's got a bit of a round wall there. My date of birth is 14th May 1909. I was five when the First World War broke out. I can remember that because I saw a chap at the top of Pound Street come out of his house and start putting flags out. That was his way of telling people that the War had started.

"Another of my earliest memories concerns Mr Dodge who had a bakery on the corner of Fore Street where the Post Office is now. He must have done a bread delivery to some district in the morning but at four o'clock in the afternoon he'd do a delivery up our way, along Pound Street and down Vicarage Street. I've got to tell you this. He had a horse and a square sort of bread cart. We kids used to sit on the stile overlooking the Common. Mr Dodge would come up with the bread cart. He used to sit us on the box on top of the cart and all the hot steam would be coming out of the bread. It was fresh baked bread. It was all hot and lovely. It was gallon loaves then with a big base and a top. For the old people Mr Dodge would take the top off the loaf so it wouldn't cost them so much. I forget how much bread cost then, it couldn't have been no more than threepence a loaf. He'd sit us on top of the cart, two or three of us boys, and give us a ride home. He'd open up the doors on the back of the van. There was like long trays with bread on, that was his afternoon bake. When he opened the doors the steam would come out and Mr Dodge would make a joke about it. He'd say 'Hooray' or something like that. Mr Dodge was a short, sort of red-faced man, he was very genial, he was fatherly like.

"I can remember when I was a boy, aged about six, I was sitting on the doorstep up Pound Street and the Salvation Army would come along on Sunday mornings and play outside Butt's Stores. At quarter to twelve they'd form up and march with a big flag, with the big drum and the trumpets playing, down to the Citadel at the Common. As they marched up Pound Street, the cornet player lived up Pound Street, so he'd drop out and go in home, then another, perhaps a bloke with a flag, would reach his house and he'd disappear. That's how it would go. By the time the band had got to the Common there were only a few players left. There was a little fellow called Peter in it and he was also in the Town Band.

"The Town Band used to play selections in the Market Place or at the top of the High Street. Mr Pearce used to carry the big drum. Little Peter used to carry a stand. When the Band got to where they wanted to play Peter would run forward and erect the stand so that Mr Pearce could put the drum on it. Peter had like a fold-up stool with a canvas seat.

"The Burgess family had two shops. One was the Post Office at Silver Street, by the Obelisk, and the other was at Pound Street. Opposite was another little teeny shop run by a lady with her old mother. Next to it, in later years, was a fish and chip shop run by the Curtis family. That was Alwyn Curtis' father.

"Molly Butt had a shop at the bottom of Pound Street. She was one of the Gregory family who used to run a private school in Vicarage Street nearly opposite St Denys'. We boys used to go down there and stand outside Molly's shop, looking in the window. We used to feast our eyes on like chocolate mice with a bit of string for the tail. There was a big ginger cat in the shop and he used to lay in the window sunning himself. That bloody cat, the blighter, used to be sprawled out on all the sweets. We used to tap on the window and shout 'Look!' but Molly never took no notice. When you went down Molly's to get any sugar or tea, she'd get a piece of brown paper, roll it up, and twist it at the bottom. It used to look like a cornet. Then she'd weigh out the sugar or the tea and tip it into the paper. You could buy stuff like that for a halfpenny a time.

"My grandparents were one of the first couples to get the old age pension in Warminster. I think that was 1912. It was 12s 6d a week for two people. That's all. I think their rent was 2s 6d a week. The old people had to live hand to mouth. It was terrible really when you look back.

"My old grandfather used to like a drop of beer. He'd send me when I was a small boy down to the Lamb pub at Vicarage Street with threepence and a jug. I'd go to the window and old man Bush, who was the landlord, would say 'Coupe down.' That was so no one would see me because I was under age. I would give him the jug and the money and get back out of sight. There was a cubbyhole where the women used to go. They'd tap on the window and get a drink but stand back out of the way so the men couldn't see them.

"There was another pub in Vicarage Street, nearly opposite the Lamb. That was the Star and Mr Weston had that. During the First World War he used to run a soup kitchen there. I used to go down there with a halfpenny and get half a jug of soup. You used to go up the back where Weston had a sort of old dairy place. They'd dip the soup out into your jug with a measure. There were quite a few soup kitchens in Warminster during the First World War. I suppose that was the same all over the country.

"I started at the Minster School when I was five. I used to walk to school from Pound Street. That's when I formed a friendship with Billy Maidment who's dead and gone now. You know his brother Herbie? Their father was killed in the First World War. I used to call at Billy's house. It's demolished now. It was one of a couple of cottages in Vicarage Street but where they stood is just a blank wall there today. Billy's mother always used to ask me in. She was a widow with three children. If Billy hadn't finished his breakfast his mother, bless her, would always ask me to have something to eat with him, a bit of toast or something. I was friends with Billy until he died. He used to work at the Reme.

"Miss Frost was the headmistress at the Minster School. I can't remember the names of the other teachers. I used to go home to dinner. I would have some soup for dinner or mother might have done a bit of baking. We didn't have much. Like all the kids in them days we went to school in our rags and tags. Some parents dressed their little boys in sailor suits. Most of us were scruffy with holes in our socks and dirty boots. That was life. Life was terrible really. Nobody thought of themselves as one up on anybody else but three or four bigger boys, if they were mates together, would pick on someone smaller in stature.

**Deverill Road (Bell Hill) in the 1930s.**

They'd aggravate like that. Same as if the younger boys were quarrelling the older ones would step in and sort it out. I went to the Minster School for just over a twelve-month and then things were changed round. Myself and some other children at the Minster School were moved to Sambourne School.

"When I went up to Sambourne School in 1919 it was a mixed school but the boys were in separate parts of the buildings to the girls. The headmaster was Jimmy Bartlett. The lady teacher was Mrs Ashman and she lived at the house at Silver Street with steps and iron railings going up to the door [The Cedars]. School commenced at nine o'clock. Five minutes before a hand bell was rung or a whistle was blown and we had to immediately form up into lines near the main doorway by the bell tower. The school gates were locked and we marched through into the long room where we sat up in the gallery. Girls would sit one side and boys the other. The smaller children were below. We had prayers and a hymn before going to our respective classrooms. I remember the hymns which were sung, first and last verses: *All Things Bright And Beautiful* and *Every Morning The Sun Rises Warm And Bright*. Mrs Ashman played the piano.

"We then proceeded to our classrooms and the register was called. Some of us had to put out the books from the cupboard. In the first standard one boy a week was teacher's boy and he had to be ink monitor, filling up the ink wells. That didn't always go down well. There was always rivalry between the boys from the Common and those from other parts of the town. Our desks were long and narrow with rough tops. We had hard seats to sit on. We did the usual sort of lessons - reading, writing and arithmetic.

"Our recreation periods were ten o'clock to quarter past ten in the morning and three o'clock to quarter past three in the afternoon. We used to rush outside. Some of us kicked a tennis ball about. The boys were divided from the girls by a large corrugated fence which stretched the full width of the school yard. We boys couldn't see the girls but we would shout out different names to see who would answer. There was always a lot of shouting and giggling but if it got too much the teacher would tell us to shut up or get away. Sometimes we'd throw a sweet or an apple over the fence to the girls.

"At 12 noon lessons stopped for dinner. Those who lived nearby went home but those who lived at the far end of Portway or Victoria Road stayed and ate food they had brought with them. That would be a bit of bread, or bread and jam, or bread and dripping. Sometimes they'd have a piece of cake or a slice of bread pudding. I believe the boys sat in the cloakroom but I've no idea where the girls ate their grub. The afternoon lessons started at two o'clock.

"We used to have to go to the dentist via the school. It's gone now but there used to be a little schoolroom in the Close. They examined you at school, you were given a card and had to take it with you down to the Close when the dentist came from Trowbridge. I had one or two teeth out. It was very frightening. The dentist wore a white coat and he had a big syringe with a needle to stick in you.

**Scottish troops marching through the Market Place during the First World War.**

Once or twice I went to the dentist but I didn't actually go in when I got there.

"If I wanted a haircut when I was a boy I was taken up to Tom Bellew's at East Street. I was too small for the chair. He used to put a stool up in the chair and I had to kneel on it. You faced the back of the chair. The style then was to have nearly all your hair cut off but have a tuft left at the front. I remember one boy saying 'I wish he'd cut that off because every time I do something wrong my old man grabs me by that tuft of hair.'

"During the First World War there were Australian, Canadian and New Zealand troops stationed in camps at Sutton Veny and the Deverills. The soldiers going off to war would march through Crockerton to the Common and on to Warminster Railway Station. They would come past Sambourne School. When we heard the army bands playing we would ask the headmaster, through the teacher, if we could go outside to see the soldiers passing by. We children would line up along the pavement outside Christ Church waving our hands and cheering. Sometimes someone would have a flag to wave. There were tables set up near the pavements where adults handed packets of cigarettes and sweets and fruit to the soldiers as they marched past. If the soldiers came along during our dinner break lots of us boys wouldn't go home to dinner. We'd march behind the soldiers down to the Town Hall and sometimes right the way to the Railway Station.

"On Saturdays different soldiers used to route march from Sutton Veny through Warminster to Longleat Park Gates, then via Cannimore and Crockerton back to Sutton Veny. Large numbers of Sambourne boys would go with them, follow behind them. They didn't tell us to push off or anything like that. They would give some of the older boys cigarettes. The Cully boys and the Fear boys from the Common used to smoke. They were older than me. Well, the boys used to go in the lavatory at school and smoke. They'd make some excuse about wanting to go to the toilet. When they got back into the class the teacher would smell the tobacco on their breath. Old Manley would cane any boy that he thought had been smoking. The boys would hang around in the playground for a bit after having a drag on a cigarette, hoping the fresh air would take the smell of the fags away. Woe betide anyone that told on a boy for smoking.

"Anyway, to get back to these soldiers route marching. When we got to camp the soldiers would say 'Come along you lads. Come on in here with us.' They let us have a meal with them. They'd find us a tin plate and we'd line up with them and grab some food. That was always a great treat. There'd be about a dozen boys tucking in. Then afterwards the soldiers would give us a bit of fruit, some oranges or apples, whatever they had. We had to walk all the way back home afterwards. We either went along the road, the long way round from Sutton Veny, via Boreham, or we cut through the Marsh. When you got to Sambourne there was no West Parade, no houses there. It was fields then. We took the path along by the Workhouse wall and that brought us out by the Shirt and Collar Factory at Pound Street.

"We knew all about the First World War. Our parents and the teachers told us things about it. We used to have flag days. We kids were issued with flags and we had to march to church on certain days. On Ascension Day we had to go to church in the afternoon. Our flags were Union Jacks and naval ones but I've no idea where they came from. They were stacked outside church while we went in for the service and we'd grab them back on the way out.

"A number of boys from Sambourne

**The funeral procession of Corporal Bodner passing along Station Road during the First World War.**

**The cast of *The Gondoliers* as presented by the Warminster Operatic Society in April 1926.**

School were choirboys. Some were at Christ Church and others at the Parish Church of St Denys', the Minster. I joined the Minster Choir during the First World War and I was in it until 1924 when my voice broke. There was always a keen rivalry between the Christ Church choirboys and the Minster choirboys. We never sang in each other's churches. In the summertime there would be a choir outing. We used to go to the park at Edington, have tea and buns, and row across the lake in boats. That was our idea of a great day out.

"When I was a choirboy, just after the First World War, they put on a play at the Palace Cinema, the old Athenaeum. It was called *Seven Days' Leave*. They wanted six choirboys to take part in the Armistice Service scene. They picked eight of us, as it happened, and they paid us sixpence each. It was only a one night stand. An elderly chap there said to me 'I'll have you.' I looked at him. I was frightened by strangers. He took me into a small room at the back of the stage and dressed me in a little sailor suit. For the play he had to go on stage in a soldier's blue uniform with his arm tied up. He had to look like he had come from a battle. They had a cross, like the Portway memorial, on stage. I had to go on stage with him. I had to act as a sailor and I was paid a shilling for that. A shilling was a lot of money then.

"The Warminster Operatic Society used to put on regular shows at the Palace, like *The Mikado* and *The Gondoliers*. They were big events. The Operatic was run by business people of the town. And round at the Minster Church they used to put on a pilgrims' thing. We used to have to wear an old sack over our clothes and black our faces, to look like pilgrims. We had to come from the toilets, at the side, while someone was playing a harmonium down in the pit. We had to sing. We got paid threepence. For being a church choirboy we got paid 1s 6d a quarter. Whatever money you got you had to take it straight home for your parents. You dared not sneak off anywhere and spend some of it or all of it. They knew at home what you had been paid and they had it. They'd give you something back but you had to take it all home first.

"Canon Jacobs, at the Minster, had some aunts who lived at the Beeches on Boreham Road. Every morning before school I had to leave home at half past six in the morning to go to the Beeches to get in the wood and coal for the aunts and clean their shoes. These old ladies were very strict. One of them would say 'There's something else I want you to do, Ingram.' I'd say 'But I've got to get to school.' I had to dash off along Chain Lane, go down over Sandy Hollow, and through the Marsh, up Upper Marsh Road, to get to school. See, remember what I said just now, they'd lock the school gates at nine o'clock. The bell tower at the school was getting a bit rickety and at five to nine the head boy from standard seven would ring a hand bell for everyone to line up in their standards. At nine the headmaster, Jimmy Bartlett, would say 'Proceed' and march everyone into the school. I used to worry like hell about being late so I ran like mad from Boreham Road to school.

"I must have been about ten years old when I started working for Canon Jacobs' aunts. They paid me half-a-crown a week. I had to take that home and hand it over. I got threepence back for myself. Two and six was a lot of money. I dared not lose it. So I used to put it in a corner of my white handkerchief, tie it in a knot, and hitch it inside my braces. It would have been the end of the world if I had ever lost that money.

"One Thursday, Ascension Day, they were going to have a church service at the Minster in the afternoon. In the

**Christ Church, pictured from the north east, 1968.
The new churchyard was consecrated by the Bishop Of Salisbury on 11 July 1909.**

morning some of the students from St Boniface College came up to school to give a lesson and then they closed the school early. I had told Canon Jacobs' aunts that I would be free in the morning and they said 'You come up to us and do a bit of gardening.' I went up. When it got to one o'clock I said to them 'I must go.' They said 'Why?' I said 'There's a service at the Minster this afternoon for the children and I have to attend. I'm in the choir.' The old lady said 'Don't bother about that, you stay here.' She kept me there until three o'clock and then she said 'You can go, I don't think there's anything else you need do here.' I nearly cried my eyes out. The church service had started at half past two. I had missed it. When I got home I said 'I'm not going up there again.' When I went up to the Beeches on the Saturday, at the end of the week, to collect my money, the old aunt said 'That's all now.' I said 'Yes, that's all now, I've finished!' She didn't like that. She told Canon Jacobs. The curate came to see me but I was adamant. That business brought home to me what the steps of society was all about. We were all down there and the higher-ups pressurised you.

"At Christ Church there was a very old gentleman who was the sexton. Most of us boys used to talk to him in his garden or in the old Christ Church Reading Room which was pulled down long ago. He was taken ill and died. Six of us choirboys felt we would like to go to his funeral. It was during the school dinner break, at half past one. We went. We all sat right at the back of Christ Church so we could creep out quietly to get back to school before two o'clock.

We lost track of time and heard, from the clock tower, the quarter chimes for quarter past two. We hurriedly raced back to school and were met by a very angry teacher. We explained what had happened and this teacher said we all had to stay in during afternoon break while he made some enquiries.

"We all thought we wouldn't get the cane but knew some sort of punishment would be administered. When class resumed at quarter past three the teacher said he would have a court held by our classmates to decide what punishment should be given. One boy was selected as judge, one boy was prosecuting counsel, and one boy would defend us. Nine boys formed a jury and the rest of the class would act as the general public. We were questioned very thoroughly and after some deliberation the verdict was that we would lose our playtime periods for the rest of the week. Next morning, when we had settled in class, the teacher told the boys that they had been fair in their verdict but Mr Bartlett, the headmaster, cancelled our decision about us losing our playtime breaks. He reckoned we had not really played truant and our attending the funeral was a noble gesture on our part.

"Those who did play truant ran the gauntlet of being dealt with by the schools' inspector. If a boy or a girl was absent from school and the parents did not notify the teacher or the headmaster then the schools' attendance officer would visit the home of the child to find out the reason. If a doctor was attending a child at home a note would be expected. I believe the inspector's name was Mr Pearce and he rode a bicycle. If a boy or a girl was seen out in Warminster during school hours without an excuse they were in serious trouble. It always meant punishment in the end.

"I must tell you about the apple stealing episode. At the top of Pound Street, where the lane led up to the recreation field, there was a high wall overlooking some gardens. To hang on to the top of the wall you had to get a toe hold in the ridge lower down. One Sunday evening four of us boys were hanging on the wall when someone said 'There's two boys up in the apple tree.' We looked and saw that one of the two boys had his shirt front all undone. He was picking apples and putting them inside his shirt. Silly-like we all started shouting things like 'Don't forget us.' Other boys stood around making quite a din. Suddenly I felt a stinging blow on my buttocks and on my legs above the back of my knees. At the same time I was wrenched violently off the wall. I soon discovered who had hit me. I turned round to see two policemen, Constable O'Shea and Constable O'Donnell, and they said sternly 'Go home immediately.' By that time the rest of the lads in the lane had vanished. The two in the tree were not so lucky.

"On the following Monday morning when I went into assembly at school there seemed to be an air of disquiet around. After prayers the headmaster, who looked terribly stern, said to the whole school 'It has come to my knowledge that some boys, few in number, have disgraced not only this school but also their parents, their church and their friends. So I am going to punish them for it.' He then called out the boys to stand in front of him, spaced apart. I was the last one on the end. Each boy was caned, starting with the two boys who stole apples from the tree. They received two canings on each hand. I was fortunate, I only got one caning on each hand. I always remember, as I was punished, the headmaster said 'I am disappointed to think you were involved with these other boys.'

"On the Friday night of the same week I went to choir practice but on going into the vestry I was told by the organist to go home. I was also told that I would not be singing in the choir on the following Sunday. I had to go to Sunday School and sit in church with the Sunday School children. I never involved myself in anything like that again and kept well out of trouble. The two boys who stole the apples also had the birch by the police.

"The most dramatic incident I recall in school was when a boy had been harshly punished by a teacher. The boy's brother was so upset he climbed over the school wall into the street and ran into town to tell his mother. She was working at the old steam laundry, the Castle Laundry, at George Street. We were all at ten o'clock morning playtime when the mother came into school with her son who pointed out to her the teacher concerned. The mother grabbed hold of the teacher by his shirt front and shook him. She tried to strangle him. Immediately all the boys hurried back into school. The police were called and the mother of the boy was summoned for assault. She appeared before the magistrates at the Town Hall and was fined one guinea or a month in prison. The Reverend Stuart, Vicar of Christ Church, paid the fine for her. An account of this was published in the *Warminster Journal* at the time.

"In 1919 they transferred the girls from Sambourne School down to the Minster and Sambourne became an all boys school. It was every boy's ambition by the time he was leaving school to be in standard seven. That was the class the headmaster took. Many did not get that far. Only above average pupils moved up each year and I can remember some 14 year olds who left school when they were still in standard four or five. When you got to the headmaster's class, standard seven, you felt you had reached the top. There were no more than 30 pupils in it and we were told that the rest of the school looked up to us. We were also told that we must never let the headmaster down. His cane always lay across his desk as a symbol of discipline. I never saw him strike a boy in anger and his judgement did not always mean the cane.

"There was a different atmosphere of relaxed learning in the headmaster's class. You were praised when you were good in any subject. Mr Bartlett kept bees in the school gardens and 16 of us boys were selected as his bee squadron. The 16 were split up into different sections. Four boys trained to use the smoke canister, four trained for the rattles, and the rest prepared the hives and collected the bees. Netted straw hats were kept in the cloakroom. You got stung. If I got stung I'd puff some of the smoke from the canister on where it did hurt. Of course a bee dies after it has stung you. Mr Bartlett used bare hands when he was handling bees. A manual honey extractor was kept and when the time came for bottling the honey there was always great excitement. It was sold to the boys for sixpence a jar. That was a lot of money in those days and boys had to save up if they wanted to buy some of the honey. And you had to bring your own jar from home.

"There were five or six hives in the front garden of the school. It was wonderful to be in Mr Bartlett's bee squadron. He taught us a rhyme: 'A swarm of bees in May is worth a load of hay, a swarm of bees in June is worth a silver spoon, and a swarm of bees in July is not worth a fly.' He used to make us repeat that rhyme.

"Very often Mr Bartlett would receive a message from the school caretaker, that had been passed on, to say that someone had a swarm of bees in their garden. When that happened, work in the classroom, no matter what lesson it was, stopped and the 16 boys of the bee squadron would go into action. They got kitted up and left the school with the headmaster. He'd get his bicycle from Teddington House at Church Street. That's where he lived. He lodged there with Miss Dredge. It was nothing unusual for people to see him pedalling off down Emwell Street and up Sambourne Road with all us boys chasing behind. Warminster was quiet then and there were very few motor cars about. Hardly any.

"Jimmy would be pedalling on his Sunbeam bicycle while the boys ran alongside and behind. They took a folding ladder with them. When they got to say, an apple tree at Henford Marsh, where the swarm had settled, the four in netted hats would collect the swarm while the four with the canisters puffed the smoke. The bees were put into a skip and taken back to a spare hive at the school. You'd get a swarm at any time in the summer. Then you'd be off to Crockerton somewhere. I remember once we collected a swarm from Mr Dowding's farm at Smallbrook. If a message about a swarm was announced at half past three you couldn't say 'Sir, I've got to go home at four.' You had to go with Mr Bartlett to see to the bees. That meant you were late home. If your dad was a rough so-and-so from down the Common you'd get a beating when you got home for being late.

"Once, Mr Bartlett announced that a farmer out Longbridge Deverill had an orchard of apple trees and we could have the fallers. We had to run out to Longbridge Deverill with him and get them. They were given to us but we had to go out and fetch them. We'd also go out on nature walks around Cannimore. We were counted as we went out of school and counted back in. No one could say 'I'm going home' when we were out. You had to go back to school. Mr Bartlett was very keen on nature. He showed us plants and told us lots of things about animals and birds.

"Jimmy Bartlett was a wonderful man. He was a sort of father figure. He was strict mind but any punishment he gave

**The Palace Cinema undergoing restoration in 1927.**

**James Bartlett, Headmaster of Sambourne School, pictured about 1919.**

had to fit the crime. Whenever there was a dispute he asked for both sides of the story. He was fair like that. The other teachers, Mr Manley and Mr Langdon, they'd come out of the army, they'd been in the First World War, and they could be vicious when they dealt out the punishment. They taught you things but you had to do as much as you could for yourself. We did a lot of drawing and reading. There were 30 odd books in the classroom, things like *Brer Rabbit*. When it came to your marks for how you spoke, how you had learnt things, you were rewarded by getting the better books, things like *Robin Hood*. If you were not so clever you got a simpler book, like one with verses in. Each class had its cupboard of books and a boy to put out the books.

"Jimmy Bartlett retired as headmaster and his place was taken by Fred Taylor who came down from up north. I can remember when the moment came for Mr Bartlett to leave Sambourne School. The Reverend Stuart came over from Christ Church and said a few words. He spoke to the school. Then we all went outside and Mr Bartlett got on his bicycle, by the steps that went down to the road. These steps are now no more because they've altered it now. We pushed Jimmy on his bicycle to give him a good start down Boot Hill and off he went to Sherborne in Dorset. That's where he went. He cycled there. That's how Jimmy left Sambourne School.

"In 1920 a shield was given by the Men's Own Brotherhood. This was to be competed for by teams of eight boys each from schools in Warminster in a race held each year on Easter Sunday. The race started at Warminster Post Office and you had to run through the Market Place, up Weymouth Street, up the hill and into the Warminster Town Football Ground. You had to run once round the field and finish at the grandstand. In 1923 I was one of the Sambourne School team and we won the shield. That was after Jimmy Bartlett had left. I think the school had won it once before.

"Talking of Easter reminds me of something. My grandfather worked for Mr Greenland who was a painter and decorator. Mr Greenland was the town bandmaster. I can remember going with father up into a room to hear the town band rehearse. Anyhow, grandfather was made a special postman. I can recall going with him one Easter, Good Friday it was, up to the farm school at the top of Folly Lane. That was the Reformatory School for Boys at Tascroft. It's converted into houses now. We went round the back and there was an elderly lady there. She had cooked a load of hot cross buns and she had put them out on the window sill. She gave me one. Coo, that was a real treat.

"The boys from the Reformatory School used to march from there down to church at the Minster on Sunday mornings. There were about 40 to 60 of them. They come all down West Street. They had their own band, all dressed in Reformatory School blue uniforms. Those boys would take up the west side of the church. The bloke in charge of those boys had come out of the army. I got linked up with him later on when he was in charge of the boys at the Warminster Timber Company.

"When I was going to Sambourne School we used to go along by the gardens, by the outside wall, and there'd be tramps laid out on the grass, waiting to go into the Workhouse. They'd go in at about half past eight in the morning, that's when the big doors would open. We'd see them as we went into the side gate into school. Those tramps had their trousers tied up with bits of string. We shuddered away from them. Of course, there was no West Parade, that was fields with farmer Greening's cows in. A path ran along the edge of the cricket pitch, what is now the back of the West Parade houses. The tramps would be hanging about there in one big batch, waiting to go in. You didn't see them down in the town. If they loitered about down there the police would pick them up for vagrancy. The police would move them on, take them out of town to say Boreham Crossroads and tell them to get on their way.

"Each town had a workhouse and there'd be something like a farthing on the rates to cover the cost. When the tramps got inside they had to chop a bit of wood or smash up some stones. If they didn't do that they couldn't stop the night and they couldn't get a meal. There used to be two old characters at Warminster Workhouse. That was old Peter and Blind Tom. They used to take chopped wood out in bundles to the shops. They had a barrow. The shops sold the wood for firewood, for three halfpence a bundle. Blind Tom used to walk in the gutter holding onto the handle of the barrow. Old Peter told him where to walk. I remember people saying that Blind Tom could recognise voices, he knew who he was talking to. Sometimes he'd use his hand to feel faces.

"During the First World War years children didn't go out to play in the streets in the evening because there were hardly any gas lamps lit and soldiers were about in the dark. Before the Alcock Crest council housing estate was built our Pound Street Recreation Field was there. It was given to the town, for the boys and girls, by Dr Alcock. He was the headmaster of the Grammar School. In the rec were large swings, small swings,

**Tascroft Court (the old Reformatory School) pictured in 1986.**

'If you be quiet and good I'll take you up into my studio.'
Claude Willcox's wireless broadcasting equipment at the Warminster Motor Company, about 1915.

see-saws and seats dotted around. Like today, all boys were football crazy and in the evenings a lot of us would play football. In the summer the rec was open until nine at night but in the winter it closed at six. Boys and girls from the Common would come up and so would boys and girls from the town. To start an evening off a football game would commence with about six town boys and six Common boys playing. As different ones came into the rec on to the field there would be shouts of 'Common here' and 'Town there'. Very soon there'd be as many as 30 kicking, pushing and sometimes fighting. Some of the older boys would break it up.

"When the rec-keeper blew his whistle to close the rec everyone came out to go home. From the outside of the playing field was a path leading through turnstiles towards the Common. At the last turnstile was the boundary between the town and the Common. One could look down the steep twisting path, which has gone now, to a small stream at the bottom in Fore Street. Town boys would sometimes go down there but at their own risk because there was always small groups of Common boys hanging about the area. If you were a town boy and you were alone when you got to the turnstile you were stopped by the Common lads. To get through you had to pay some kind of forfeit. That could be two cigarette cards, an apple, or some sweets. If you had nothing on you, well, you had to promise to pay the next day at school. You had to keep your promise. If you were in a group of 'townies', as the Common boys used to call us, you could get past the stiles without paying by pushing and punching.

"When you read or you hear someone saying that the Common was rough you can accept that as true. It was rough right up until the time I got married. I'll give you an instance. During the First World War the Australian soldiers used to get in the Globe. That was their pub. A fight broke out down there between the Aussies and some of the blokes from the Common. This is when there were some railings by the steps outside. A soldier got injured and died not long afterwards. It wasn't deliberate, it was an accident. One of the blokes from the Common was implicated. He got out of Warminster after that. He went to Wales to work in the coal mines.

"The thing with the Common was that all the families down there were closely related. It was so integrated. Like the Cliffords, the Grists, the Smiths, and the Vincents and the Prices. If ever there was any trouble, even though those people never got on well with themselves, they would close ranks. If you upset anyone you upset the lot. Well, the policemen used to go down there in pairs. Never one on his own, always two together.

"I can remember when the women at the Common used to wash their clothes in the stream. It's piped in now but the brook used to run alongside the road. Hillwood was always known as Viper's Island. Once a year the villagers from Crockerton would come in and have a fight with the Commoners at Viper's Island. They'd use big staves. They'd hammer one another to pieces. The police kept out of the way of that. They only went in to bring out the casualties. That's true. That fight used to take place on a certain day in the summer. I was wary of the Common. It was dicey. If you went through there you hurried. It was usually best to go out around it.

"When we were young, going to school or out playing, we wore the one pair of hobnail boots that we had. Mine were bought from Dodge's shop at George Street for 2s 6d. Those boots used to make my heels sore around the ankles. Playing football your boots got scuffed. Then they had to be repaired with new hobs and bits of leather. You ended up with patchwork boots. The play yard at Sambourne School was rough, like the Pound Street rec, and if you got kicked in the leg playing football you were kicked by a hobnail boot. That hurt. Our football was one of they old-fashioned ones, leather, and it was done up with lace.

"Lots of the lads I played football with as a boy went on to play for Christ Church, and Warminster Town, and Warminster Reserves. I can remember the Vincents, the Elloways, the Turners, all of them. Haines went on to play for Portsmouth. That's why I think how great it is, Danny, when I see the old photographs you publish of them teams and those people. It brings back so many memories.

"Lots of people used to go and watch football at the Town Ground. There was a little hut that held about 60 people and the Committee used to get in there. The toilets up in the corner were just a tin place. The players had no changing facilities. They had to go home, if it had been raining, soaked through. There was a fellow called Pinnell lived up West Street and he used to carry the netting and about six or seven footballs to the matches. Mr Mills was the secretary. We kids used to go to the matches but we couldn't afford to go in before the start. It was twopence. Some of the Secondary School boys could afford that but we couldn't. We had to wait outside. At half time they'd let us in for free. If you saw someone you knew paying to go in at the start your first thought was 'Where the hell did he get twopence from? He must have pinched it.'

"I remember once we were playing in the Pound Street rec, one summer evening, it was about half past six, and I noticed some smoke. That was the Mineral Water Factory at Emwell Street on fire. I shouted 'There's a fire!' and we all chased off down Emwell Street to see what was happening. Some went Pound Street way and others went up Sambourne. The fire brigade was there. I think Mr Dewey was in charge. He was captain. The firemen had their brass helmets on. The factory was blowing up and falling down. The bottles had marbles in the necks and they were exploding and going off in all directions. Tommy Sharp lived opposite in one of the two houses and the windows were getting smashed in by the pops and bangs. The fire brigade had a horse drawn tender. They used to harness the horses up in Button's Yard at East Street. They used Mr Button's horses which were kept in a field up Smallbrook. The fire station was in the Close. To us kids the firemen always seemed to be elderly men with whiskers and beards.

"I remember being up Boreham Road one day and I could hear an army band coming. That was a funeral procession. A soldier had died. They were carrying him in his coffin on a horse drawn wagon from Sutton Veny, up Boreham Road, to the Railway Station. He was escorted by the band. The soldiers were walking in their great coats and I couldn't understand why they were carrying their rifles under their arms. Of course, there was a big 'flu' epidemic out Sutton Veny during the First World War. It swept through the huts, the prisoner of war camp, and the village. A lot of soldiers who died of the 'flu' are buried in Sutton Veny Churchyard.

"To get a few pennies to go to pictures on Saturday afternoons, four of us would go out to Gas House, off Bath Road, in the morning. The old folk from Pound Street and elsewhere would have 28lbs of coke from Gas House. They'd pay us a farthing or a halfpenny to go and collect their coal. Except one old lady, Mrs Player, who lived up the top of Pound Street. She never ever gave us money. She used to make toffee. Instead of giving us money she'd break a piece of this toffee out of the tray. We'd take our trolleys and our sacks to get the coke. The old chap at Gas House would weigh it out for us. The eldest boy would pay him the money. I think coke was about two bob. After we had delivered the coke we would pool our money.

"We would go into Burgess' shop and post office at the end of Silver Street and get a great big piece of pudding with currants in, for a farthing, They used to have it in the window. They cut it up in big slabs. Then we'd go up to the corner of the Town Hall and Weymouth Street. They used to have stalls on the side of the road there on Saturday afternoons. From there we'd get a halfpennyworth of broken biscuits and a bottle of lemonade for a penny. That was the old bottles with the marble codswallop in the neck. We'd be left with a penny to go in and see the pictures in the Palace. That's the Athenaeum Arts Centre now.

"We'd watch silent films put on by Albany Ward. That were like a madhouse in there. It was full of kids. The seats near the front were in a dip and they'd come back, upwards, towards the stalls at the rear. If you were at the back you'd sit on top of the seats otherwise you couldn't see. When part one of the programme ended you were in pitch black darkness. There'd be hollering and shouting. Boys would be throwing things and the floor was all covered in orange peel and paper. They had a piano accompaniment to the films. Mrs Minhinnick played. She'd come in and sit up by the curtain. She played fast where there was some action going on and slow when it was a quiet

**Arn Hill, 1934. Southdown House is visible and just one house (bottom left) on the Westbury Road.**

part. If there was a river scene she'd play some water music.

"Cecil Eacott, from up top of Pound Street, was a helper at the Palace. He'd come in with a torch. He had a stick to tap anyone that was doing something naughty. If anyone got violent he'd chuck them out. In between films, while they were changing the reels, we boys would get a bit of a commotion going. We'd tell Cecil that one of the boys had done something. We'd say 'It were him, it were him.' Then someone would get dragged out. The films went on from about half past two to half past four. It was mostly Charlie Chaplin and things like that.

"I'll tell you about another thing I used to do on Saturday mornings. I used to go to Fred Owen's up Portway and sit on his steps, to wait for him. Fred Owen lives up the Ridgeway now. When he came out he and I would go up to Arn Hill and sit on the bank outside the little golf hut.

George Gilbert's father used to run that. The Gilberts lived by the pub in East Street. We would sit by the hut and people would come up to play golf. Someone would say 'Boy, I want a caddy.' We'd caddy, carrying the clubs, and you'd get sixpence for doing nine holes. I used to go back and do another round in the afternoon. Fred, living down just below at Portway, would go home at dinner time and come back with some sandwiches for me. He and I were very friendly. After a while, doing the caddying, you got to know about the various golf clubs. Sometimes you could say to one of the men playing, when he got to a certain hole, 'You need a number four iron, sir.' You got to know all about that.

"Percy Pearce at West Street, I think he's dead now, when we were about to leave Sambourne School, had a fixed wheel bike with solid tyres which he used to ride to school. You had to keep pedalling and to stop you had to back pedal a little bit. All the boys wanted to have a go on it. West Parade had just been built. I remember we came out of school. Someone had a go on Percy's bike and then Percy said 'Go on, Len, you have a go but don't forget you've got to back pedal to stop.' I went along West Parade but when I got to the end, to Pound Street, Percy didn't say turn left and I went straight into the brick wall of a villa there. I think an insurance agent lived there. I fell off. Percy was only worried about his bike. He said 'You're not going to get on there again.'

"I left school when I was 14, in 1923. Prior to leaving school, after I had left my part time job with Canon Jacobs' aunts, I had been going on Saturday mornings to work at Mr Claude Willcox's house in George Street. Claude Willcox was a successful businessman. He had the Warminster Motor Company at the other end, the west end, of George Street. There were only five cars in Warminster when I worked for Claude Willcox. That was Lord Bath's, a couple of doctors', a farmer's and someone else's.

"Claude Willcox lived next door to Butcher's Yard. His house is a chemist's shop now. He had a housekeeper, who used to live in Emwell Street. She used to cook the meals and I used to serve Mr Willcox at the table. I had to wear a little white coat. The director of the Motor Works would come to dinner. The lady taught me how to serve correctly. I can't remember her name. She was going to leave Warminster and she wanted to take me away with her, to be a page boy, to wait on tables and all that, but my family wouldn't allow it. I was only a boy. I used to get half a crown for a Saturday. When I left school I started going daily as my full time job. I think I got five shillings a week. That was a big sum of money.

"After the lady left Warminster, Miss Low, who had Corrymore, the big house on the corner of George Street and Ash Walk, came on the scene. Miss Low took over and she had a big say on how Mr Willcox's house was run. She could hire and fire. One day the doorbell went and I answered the door. It was a woman with a young girl. The woman said 'Is Miss Low in?' I said 'Yes.' The woman said 'Will you tell her we're here, we are expected.' What I didn't know was that the girl was coming for an interview with Miss Low, for my job! At the end of the week Miss Low paid me my wages and I was paid off. I was out and the girl took my place. Just like that. Mr Willcox had no say in the matter. He paid Miss Low to run his house and she wanted a girl not a boy.

"Claude Willcox had the first wireless broadcasting station in Warminster. On Sunday night, between half past seven and half past eight, there was a recital of music by the BBC. I used to go from choir, from the Minster Church down through Ash Walk to the Motor Works. Mr Claude used to leave the door ajar. I would go in, just pressing the bell as I went through the door and sit in a big armchair. There was a big speaker beside the chair. I'd sit and listen. That went on for some time. I used to like that.

"One night Claude said to me 'Are you interested in wireless?' I said 'Yes.' He said 'If you be quiet and good I'll take you up into my studio.' That's where he used to do his own broadcasting. He did a programme called *Warminster Calling*. I went up there. The room was nothing but wires here and wires there. I had to sit in the corner, a kind of safety zone, where it wasn't so muddled. He had a big wireless set on the table with a microphone which he spoke into. He played a certain march to start his programme. By about half past nine I was getting a bit restless and he said to me 'I think you're getting tired. You had better go on home.' He took me down to the door. In those days it was only gas lamps in the streets and you couldn't see your hand in front of your face at night. The police station was at Ash Walk, near the Motor Works, and if a policeman was about he used to take me home to Pound Street.

"Later on I had a little cat's whisker set of my own. And up at the top of Pound Street lived Jack Giles who's dead and gone now. His garden was the other side of the wall where we had been caught when the other boys had been stealing apples. Out there Jack had a shed. When he had the light on you could see the light shining through cracks in the wall. Jack had a one-valve wireless set in the shed. He invited me, George Wright and Eddie Tinnams into the shed to listen to Henry Hall's late night music show. We were listening. It was about quarter to eleven at night. There were some police houses at the top of Pound Street. Two policemen out in the road, were going on duty, and they heard the music. They crept into the garden and came into the shed. That was O'Shea and O'Donnell who lived up Pound Street. They said 'What's on in here then?' It frightened me to death. Jack said 'We're listening to the wireless.' They pointed to us boys and said 'Who are these?' They asked us our names. We told them. They said 'You better go home.' They told Jack to shut the wireless off. You had to do what they said.

"My old friend Nelson Gay, who lived down at the Obelisk Terrace, liked music. At the time I had a little portable gramophone. Nelson's father had a piggery at Trowbridge and he'd go off in a car down to there in the evenings, and his mother worked at the Bath Arms or somewhere. I said to Nelson 'I'll bring my gramophone down to your place on Saturday night.' I went down and we had the music on. Nelson said 'Why don't we dance?' We had a bit of a dance. Half past ten came round and Nelson said 'Father will be home in a moment.' I said 'That'll do for tonight.' We had a cup of cocoa and I set off up Vicarage Street for home. I was creeping up past St Denys' Convent when a voice from somewhere said 'Hello sonny, who are you?' I nearly wetted my trousers. That was a policeman.

"He said 'What have you got there?' I said 'A gramophone.' I said 'It's mine.' He said 'Where do you live?' I told him. He said 'I'll come home with you, I've got to look into this.' He thought I had stole it. I told him how I had been to see a friend at Obelisk Terrace. He asked me what was the name of the friend and what number he lived at. I couldn't remember if Nelson lived at six or eight. I got confused. I got the wrong number. This policeman said 'I don't think the Gay family live there.' That roused his suspicions. He took me home and made sure I was telling the truth. You couldn't get away with nothing with the police years ago.

"I enjoyed my time with Claude Willcox. He was typical of his time, he was very pleasant, he was quiet. He got about quiet and he spoke quiet. I suppose that's how he was brought up. See, years ago the rule was you didn't speak to anyone older than you unless they spoke first and you had to speak civil and quiet to them. I'll give you an instance of that. My old grandmother used to be friendly with a very old lady up at Pound Street. She was about 80. She used to have the Sunday supplement of the *Christian Times*. My grandmother said 'Take the supplement up to the old lady. Knock on the door and when she says come in you go in. As soon as you stand inside, you take your hat off, and don't speak to her. When she speaks to you give her the paper.' I think the old lady's name was Mrs Ponting. She used to give me a sweet, a toffee. I'd come out and put my hat back on.

"No, years ago you never accosted anyone. You never spoke to them unless they spoke to you first. The higher classes ignored you. If they did speak to you, well, you had to say 'Yes sir' or 'Yes ma'am.' And if you were walking along and someone, ladies, came towards you, you had to get off the pavement and pass them in the road. You never got up against the wall. That would have been bad manners.

"There was another golden rule and I often think about this. If you went into someone's house and you were asked to sit down, you always had to sit farthest away from the person. You didn't have to look down at ladies' ankles. Oh no. My old grandmother used to wear about three petticoats under her dress, and her dress was always black. And you never stared at anyone. You always had to look away. That was manners.

"I remember once Arthur Viney's father, who was something to do with the Minster Church, sent me with a note to Mr Harraway's at Silver Street. Mr Harraway lived in the house with the steps going up either side of the door [the Cedars]. Some while after Mr Harraway told my grandmother how well spoken I was. We boys had to talk properly. We were always brought up straight. That was the times.

"Having been pushed out of Claude Willcox's by Miss Low, I had to find some other work. There was a place up Copheap Lane and that was the Ex-Servicemen's Industries. It was a British Legion workplace. Through Cyril Titt I got a job there. I had a frame thing, dipping chairs into a solution and then turning them out to dry. There were about 50 ex-service men working there. Then, so many of the British Legion blokes had to finish. There wasn't enough work. I had to finish.

"I went down to the Warminster Timber Company, on the corner of Fairfield Road and Imber Road, as a sawyer's mate. The summer that year was beautiful. We used to finish the morning's work at twelve or one o'clock. Us boys and chaps would shoot off on bicycles down over the Hollow to Smallbrook, to where the old sewage pumping station, the Jam Factory, was. Down there they had part of the River Wylye blocked off. We'd all get in there and have a swim in our dinner hour. Then we'd get out, get dried off, get dressed and go back to work. A gang of us used to do that.

"I got married on 31st July 1928. I met my wife Daisy when I was in the choir at the Minster Church. She wasn't born in Warminster. She was born at Market Square in Poplar, up in London. She and I went back there after the Second World War to have a look round and everything she knew as a child was flattened. It was all built upon with big buildings.

"Daisy had brothers and sisters, I think there were ten or 11 of them, and she was the youngest. Some of her brothers and sisters died, leaving seven of them when her dad died. He was a widower. You see, she lost her mum when she was two years old, and she lost her dad when she was nine. Her eldest sister wasn't stupid but she wasn't quite all there. Her sister's brain wasn't all that good but she was kind enough to look after those kids for a while. She took care of their house.

"Daisy was looked after by her eldest sister for not quite two years. Then the sister went into a home. Shortly after that the next eldest sister went to work in service. Daisy then went to live with her brother but not for long. She was 11 when she was sent to the Orphanage of Pity at West Street, Warminster. The Orphanage in Warminster was connected with the Church in London. The sisters in

London arranged for her to come to Warminster.

"She found it was quite a change coming from London to Warminster. She thought Warminster was nice because she liked the country. When she was in London all the children, when they went to school, could pay towards a fortnight's holiday as a school group to the countryside. That's what used to happen to her but she never came Warminster way on that.

"Of course, there was no freedom for her when she came to Warminster. She was in the Orphanage and she couldn't go out and see places and play with other children. She had to do what the Sisters from St Denys' Convent who ran it said. The girls in the Orphanage had a summer uniform and a winter uniform, so they couldn't run away. They'd be recognised. The uniform was a red one in the winter and a blue one in the summer. They wore their summer uniform until October and then their winter one until about May. When they outgrew their uniform it was handed down to the smaller children.

"If they went out, to go to school or church, they had to walk two by two with the sisters behind them. And they'd walk in twos back to the Orphanage afterwards. They only met other children to talk and play with when they were at school. The girls wore ribbons in their hair because they had long hair. That was big bows of ribbon. I used to pinch the ribbon out of Daisy's hair. Me, Tommy Sharp, Bill Maidment, Fred Owen, Charlie Taylor, and one or two others, were always chasing after the girls.

"Daisy used to get ribbed something rotten when she got back home to the Orphanage. They'd say 'Where is your ribbon?' She knew who had it but she used to say 'I don't know.' Every Sunday I would pinch her ribbon. Somebody who lived up Sambourne way saw me pinching her ribbon one Sunday. When I went into Sambourne School on the Monday morning, the teacher, Mr Manley, said to me 'I want you.' Mr Manley gave me the cane.

"Daisy loved children and in the Orphanage there were seven kids all under the age of five. She was picked to look after them. She used to put all their clothes away. She was always very tidy, she still is now. She'd put the pants, frocks and petticoats into little piles. She had it so tidy you could open the drawer and know where anything was. Every time they had, I forget what they called it, but on certain church days the high-up people from Boreham Road, the people with money, used to go and visit the Orphanage. There'd be a proper tea for the guests. Lady Pelly was one and Mrs David Waddington, the auctioneer's wife, was another. There were church people and the members of the Board of Guardians. Afterwards the visitors were shown around. If there were any new ones in the party they were shown absolutely everything. The sisters would open the drawers and show these ladies how Daisy had arranged the little kids' clothes. Those ladies would be amazed. They couldn't make out how Daisy, a kiddy just 11 years old, could be so methodical and tidy.

"Daisy was in the Orphanage at West Street for five years. The most number of children in there was 24. As they grew older and left school they sent them out into service to work for high-up people with money. There was no choice in it. They were pushed out. While they were in the Orphanage the sisters taught the children to do the housework, the cleaning, washing, cooking and cleaning of boots. That was to prepare them for work outside when they were old enough.

"Daisy always remembers how once a month they used to have a big gammon of ham. Some of the orphans had to take a pram up to Chinn's the butchers in the

Market Place and get that big gammon of ham. They'd take it back to the Orphanage in the pram. They'd also get a bag of bones for soup. That gammon lasted about three days and those bones used to last them nearly all week. The gammon was cut and they had a little bit, only a little bit, on bread. Daisy reckons the food was nice there but it was all plain. It wasn't like what she had been used to. When she first went there, for the first fortnight she cried herself to sleep every night. It wasn't home for her but afterwards she got on alright. When she got used to it, when she realised she had to stay there and be with all the other kids and do what they did.

"As I said earlier, when they were 14 or 15 years old, old enough to go into the outside world and earn their keep, the sisters of St Denys' sent them off to work in service. They sent them to work for the gentry. Daisy's sister was in service as a parlourmaid for the Bishop of Chelmsford and they claimed her. She went to work in London for the Bishop of Chelmsford as a housemaid. She got ditched from there because she sauced them. She answered back. Then she went on for a lady who was a big pianist in the West End. The lady never paid Daisy for three months. See, these gentry didn't want to pay you. Daisy was supposed to earn £13 a year, that's £1 a month. She had her food provided, her meals and her bed, but she had to buy her clothes and everything else out of her wages. Daisy went back to her sister's place in Poplar. Although Daisy was working in service in London she did return occasionally to Warminster and that's how we picked up, we started going out together and we got married.

"When I was working at the Timber Company the wife was expecting our son Kenny. Someone gave us a lot of beetroot and she cooked it. As I was going off to work one morning she said

**The Cedars,
the former home of Mr Harraway,
at Silver Street, 1987.**

'When you come home for tea you can have beetroot and ham.' When I got home for tea I couldn't see nothing on the table. I said to her 'How are you today?' She said 'Not too bad.' I said 'Where's the tea, where's the beetroot?' She had cooked a big dish of beetroot and ate the bloody lot! She'd got one of those eating fads that pregnant women get. She used to love beetroot.

"The Timber Company had a big traction engine called *The Pride of Wiltshire* and the men used to go out getting timber, bringing it back to the works to be cut up. It took all morning for them to get that engine stoked up ready for a journey. You always knew when they were going long distance because they hitched up a little hut on the back of the carriage. That hut was the men's home while they were away from Warminster. There were also stables, where they kept the horses that pulled the timber wagons. I remember all that. One of the Bridewell family was a horseman at the Timber Company. After a while I went on cutting out wooden seats on the machine. I became a machinist. I got sixpence an hour with a bonus on every 12 seats that I cut out. I cut out the centres and passed them on to the Penn family who did the next stage in the chairmaking process.

"This was the late 1920s. There was a by-election. The sitting member died I think. Two candidates put up, a Conservative and a Liberal. There was no Labour Party candidate then. The Liberal man got in. The owners and directors of the Timber Company didn't like that. If a Conservative got in they would blow the factory hooter in triumph but not this time. Because a Liberal got in they laid off the last 12 blokes they had took on. They gave them the sack. I was one of them. Major John, who used to live in Woodcock House, was a director of the Timber Company and he was responsible for laying them blokes off. That's how things went on years ago.

"I went on the dole, I had some stamps on my card. In fact I've still got all my original cards and stuff. After a period on the dole you had to get so many stamps on your card to carry on claiming dole. You had to go every morning to sign on at the Labour Exchange. It was in the Market Place, about where John the Butcher is now. You had to go up there. They gave you a green card. Certain jobs would come up. One was when they started to lay electricity between Bristol and Salisbury and Southampton. There was some of this work going on at Heytesbury, about four miles east of Warminster. I had a green card and off I went to see about a job on the electric. You won't believe this but several other blokes and I ran from Warminster out to Heytesbury. The foreman in charge was called Ireland. He was a big fellow and he only had one eye.

"He put me on the job, doing boxing up. An old chap would stride out so many yards and I had to tidy things up for the pipes to go through. If what he strided out kept you there until five o'clock you had no choice but to stay and do it. On Wednesdays they gave you a sub of five shillings. That was to ensure you stayed working there for the rest of the week. On the Saturday you got the rest of your money, six shillings. That's all you had to come. You had to pay 1s 7d for a stamp out of your wages. It doesn't sound much but it was a lot out of your money.

"About the same time the road from Salisbury Plain was being made up, being cut through for the army, and there were a load of Irish labourers working on that. The next thing we knew a charabanc load of these Irish blokes turned up on our job and offered to work for as little as five pence per hour. There was Tom Ferris and other Warminster chaps along with me. They're all dead and gone now. When a certain stretch was done we were finished. It seemed as if they got rid of the local people on the job. I had to go back on the dole.

"My wife, Daisy, was expecting our second baby, Jean. I couldn't get enough stamps on my card to claim dole. I could go hay-making on a farm but the farmer would only pay your sick stamp, not your employment stamp. The sick stamp was ninepence and the other was 11 pence. 1s and 8d the two but they would only pay one. I went all over town to try and get a job but there was nothing doing. I ended up with a great big list of places I had tried. I didn't go back to the Timber Company to try for a job, well, I said to the wife at the time what's the point of asking Major John when he sacked me before.

"After six months I had to go before a board. The Board was at Trowbridge and I was sent a postal order for two shillings to pay for my bus fare to Trowbridge and back. I had to go to a place not far from the church and vicarage in Trowbridge. The clerk came out and he spoke to me and some of the other chaps who were waiting to go before the Board. He read out a list of who was sitting on the board. Then he asked 'Any of you got any objections?' Major John was one of the men sitting on the board. I said 'Yes. I've got an objection. I don't wish to have Major John sitting.' Major John had to come off the Board, he had to go into an ante-room.

"I went before the Board. Everyone sitting on the Board asked me loads of questions. I showed the Chairman of the Board the list of places that I had tried for jobs. He looked all down it and passed it to the others to see. They said 'Yes, you've done your best to try and get a job.' The Chairman asked if any of them had any more questions. One said 'Oh, just one. Why didn't you go back and ask you previous employer, Major John, for a job?' That was he who I had made come off the Board. I was stumped. I didn't know what to say. They said 'Go out and wait in the ante-room, we'll tell you our decision before you go.' I went and sat down. It was five o'clock. Then one of them came out and said 'Mr Ingram, we regret to say that your dole has been stopped.' I felt bloody terrible. I got outside and caught the bus on the corner. I was gutted. I had no work, I had tried and there was no jobs. I had no money and they had stopped my dole. I was married, I had a child, the wife was expecting, and I had no job and no dole. I was in tears by the time I got home. I cried to my wife.

"We were living at Cole's Buildings. I didn't know what to do. I went to see Cyril Titt. He was our insurance agent at the Co-op. He said 'I'll see what I can do.' He got about six shillings for my wife. I went to see Mr Doel at Portway. He was on the British Legion. He got us some meat and some coal. He got us a chit to say we could get some bread from Payne's. It all seems so silly when you think a quarter of corned beef was only three halfpence and eggs were a penny each. We couldn't even afford that. My uncle out Crockerton had a big smallholding with chickens and he allowed us eggs and chicken cheap. So we were able to dodge along.

"Bob Hill had a little farm at West Street. We used to get our milk off him. He came round Pound Street, Vicarage Street and West Street delivering. He'd dip the milk out of the can on the cart into your little jug. The milk was near enough straight from the cow. Hygiene! To make ends meet we used to stand the milk and take the cream off the top. We'd knock some of it up to make a little bit of butter.

"It always seemed like we were all down there. You knew your class, your station in life. Like, our class never had a table-cloth on the table. If you were to put a cloth on the table someone would say 'Who are you expecting? Is someone coming?' That's how it was. I can remember going into houses where people did have a table-cloth on the table. They never asked you to sit down. Never. As soon as what you had called for was seen to they would show you the door. They were anxious to get rid of you.

"Charlie Curtis is dead and gone now but he was a lovely bloke. His mother was a lovely person too. Charlie's widow, Ann, is still about. Charlie and I cycled to London. I had relations in London and I thought I would go and see them, to see if I could get some work up

**'There'd be a proper tea for the guests.'**
Sisters and nurses at St Denys' Convent, about 1920.

---

there. I wanted to do something to help my wife and children. (I had only been to London once before, when I was 11. My grandfather's sister died in London, intestate, and she had a bit of money. My grandad and his other sister who married Mr Crouch out Sutton Veny had the estate. That was the first time I, as a boy, saw a white five pound note).

"Charlie said he would come to London with me. I didn't have a bike but Charlie went off and got me one from somewhere. We set off on our bikes just after six o'clock one Saturday morning. We went from Warminster, up Sack Hill, through Imber to the Devizes road. We went partly into Devizes to where an aunt of Charlie's lived. She gave us a cooked breakfast. We cycled on from there and got to the centre of London, Nelson's Column, at ten past six in the evening. We were stranded there. We didn't know where we were. We wanted north London. Buses kept coming by us. One of the busmen said 'Where are you going?' We told him. He said 'Follow my bus.' We followed the bus so far until he stopped and told us where to turn off.

"We stayed at my relations. On the Monday morning we went to the nearest Labour Exchange and got our cards stamped. We told them we were looking for work, odd jobs. They said 'We've got a waiting list. You're from the country. What can you do?' They had nothing for us. They thought we were only suitable for farm work and where do you do that in London? We stayed with my relations until the Tuesday and then cycled back to Warminster. It took us from six o'clock in the morning until quarter to eight at night to get back. And it was raining, pouring. The next morning I couldn't get out of bed. I was stiff from head to toe. I had the doctor. He said I had tore myself to pieces.

"Bunny Wyatt had a shop at Silver Street. His wife looked after it. They had fish, fruit and old clothes, the stuff the gentry cast off, on sale in there. There were heaps of like jumble clothes all over the floor in Bunny's shop. When it came to my daughter Jean's christening I didn't have a suit of clothes. I went down to Bunny's. I told Mrs Wyatt my situation. She said 'I'll fix you up.' She sold me a black pair of striped trousers and a black jacket, and a nice shirt. When people, the neighbours, saw me dressed up like that they didn't want nothing to do with me. I was out on a limb. They got about, the old ladies did, in long dresses. They knew I was on the dole and they wondered where I had got the money from to buy a suit like that. What they didn't know was it cost me no more than five bob. That suit, apparently, had belonged to some bloke in the theatre world.

"Mrs Wyatt came from a theatrical background herself. She was a funny little woman, she was a dry old stick. She always wore lots of beads and stuff like that. She painted her face up with rouge and wore long ear-rings. She'd get outside the shop. Somehow she'd find out your kids' names and she'd say 'Hello Kenneth' or whatever. She'd give the little kids a kiss. She was ever so good with children. I don't think she and Bunny had any children of their own. They were elderly.

"The wife and I, with our son, Ken, would go shopping up town every Saturday. If we could find sixpence we'd go to the pictures at about half past five. We'd come out about half past seven. On Saturday night, on the corner of Weymouth Street was five stalls with groceries, vegetables, and nearly new clothes. If we had some money and we saw something we fancied we'd buy it. Then we'd head for home but on the way we'd go in Bunny Wyatt's. Bunny was

**Piccadilly Circus, London.**

always sat on an orange box outside his shop watching the people go by.

"One night Bunny shouted out to my wife 'Come on mother, your little lad wants a banana.' Kenny did like bananas, well, so did our other son Bobby. So, we stood there for a minute. I said 'We can't afford it.' Bunny said 'Of course you can.' The wife said 'How much are they then?' They were about six pence a pound or something like that. The wife said 'I can't afford to spend sixpence on one boy.' Bunny said 'Come here.' He gave my wife three bananas. He said 'That should be threepence but you can have them for a penny.' She gave him a penny. Another night Bunny said 'How about a nice bit of fish, haddock, for your supper?' Gosh, that was threepence or fourpence. He had it slapped in an old orange box. He wrapped it in a bit of ruddy newspaper. We were thrilled to bits with that. We went home, cooked it, and ate it for supper.

"My wife was able to cope on the domestic front. Before marriage the wife had worked for Dr Blackley's wife, in the big house at West Street, as a cook. She had worked over at Sutton Veny as a cook. She had learned to be a cook when she was an orphan in St Denys' Orphanage and she had been up to London working. One day I went over to Horningsham on my bicycle to do a bit of hay-making for a farmer and he fed me while I was out there. While I was out Horningsham Dr Blackley's wife came to our house and saw what my wife was preparing for dinner. She was terribly upset. In the evening Dr Blackley came up. He said 'Mr Ingram, I ascertain that you are looking for work.' I said 'Yes.' He said 'I've got a job for you up at Beckford Lodge, the hospital run by Dorset County Council, at Gipsy Lane. They want a porter. Would you like it?' I said 'Oh good gosh, yes please.' That was three years after I had applied for dole.

"I went up to Beckford Lodge as hospital porter moving the patients about. The matron told me the secretary would send me a letter with regards what wages I would get. My pay was £2 17s a week. I nearly cried. I couldn't believe how lucky I was. At the same time Butcher's were putting the new central heating system into Beckford Lodge. Mr Turner, whose wife was the caretaker at Sambourne School when I was a boy going there, was in charge for Butcher's at Beckford. He got talking to me. He said 'What's it like, working here?' I said 'I get £2 17s a week.' I forget who the bloke was who was stood with us but Turner turned round and said to him 'George, listen to this, I'm foreman for Butcher's and I get £2 13s a week, and this young man is getting £2 17s a week from Dorset County Council.'

"My first wage payment was a cheque. By that time I owed Ken Butcher's father and the milkman, and the doctor. See, if you had the doctor out you had to pay about sixpence a call. I suppose I owed £30 in total which was a hell of a lot of money. Ken Butcher's father used to come and collect sixpence a week off us, so did all the other people. We lived hand to mouth on nothing for three years and ran the bills up. Our rent was three shillings a week. Coal was 1s 11d a cwt. We had to owe for everything we had. When I got a job at Beckford I felt like I was in clover but it was some while before we paid off everybody that we owed money to.

"A lot of Warminster people were against the hospital because Dorset were using it as a TB hospital. Some locals feared that TB would spread. We used to burn the old stuff in an incinerator up the top of the garden, at the back, where Wheeler's, the nursery people, used to do bird-starving. There were no bungalows up there then. There were some houses up Gipsy Lane. Time went on. In 1936 they were running short of nurses and other positions. I was asked if I would like to be a nursing orderly. I said 'Yes.' I had to have a medical examination. I passed. When I joined the nursing staff, each morning when I went into work on the wards, my fingernails were examined for dirt. You had to be thorough with your cleanliness. I went round the wards serving breakfast to the patients and I had to shave the men.

"The area around Beckford Lodge was very quiet. If you looked out of the windows you didn't see many people. The only folks you saw outside were the Dowding family working at Smallbrook Farm. They'd be out in the fields haymaking and getting the cows in. There used to be a footpath that went down across there to Boreham. The farm has gone now and the fields are now the Prestbury Park housing estate.

"The time to see Warminster full of people was when the funfair came to town. They were lovely times. The fair was lovely when it was held in the street all up through town. We used to take our boy Kenny to it. There was nothing like the pushchairs the girls have got today. You either had a rickety old thing or you carried your kids in your arms. I carried Kenny. On the corner by the Athenaeum, when the fair was on, they'd have a great big roundabout there. Just in the Close is where they had the big steam engines that drove the roundabout. That's all Kenny wanted to see, those engines. He didn't care for the fair. He liked the engines.

"Then Kenny decided he wanted a ride on the roundabouts. My wife went on the big horses, that went up and down, with him and he screamed his bloody head off. It made the wife nervous as hell. She said 'I don't like it, I'll have to get off.' The roundabout operator said 'I can't stop it now.' The wife said 'You'll have to hold the kid then.' The operator had to hold both the wife and Kenny in his arms while the roundabout spun round. I was watching from over the road and it frightened me to death. I thought all three of 'em were going to fall off any minute. I said to the wife 'You'll never go on there again.'

"During the First World War they held the funfair up by Christ Church and they had the sheep fair on the football ground at Weymouth Street. We used to come out of school, in October, to see it. Hampton & Rowland used to have the whales, that was the big attraction. The first ride on that at four o'clock in the afternoon was a free one. There'd be about 200 kids trying to get on it. You thought the bloody thing would never start. The rides were normally threepence but that was a lot of money.

"We used to take the kids up Fairfield Road to see the cattle market. That was a big do up there. The wife went up there one day and came back with a ruddy puppy dog she'd bought for sixpence. She couldn't resist it. We had that right up until we lived in one of the houses at Woodcock, opposite where Kingdown School is now. The dog started following the soldiers into the camp. That's how we lost it. The dog followed the soldiers into the camp one day and never came back.

"I was in the Territorials. I joined it in 1928 when they had their first recruiting drive. I can remember the chaps who were in that. There was Paddy Miles, Sergeant-Major Partridge, Fred Taylor, and several chaps from out the villages. When I came back from the TA camp in August 1939 I had my call up papers for the army. I had to go down to the Drill Hall, I was made up in the ranks, and I had to issue out kit to the boys going away. We went to Tidworth, and then we went down on the coast.

"When we came back off the coast I got appendicitis. They took me to London, just off Windsor, and operated on me. They did the operation underground. I told them I had suffered problems with my stomach before and they wouldn't cut me in the usual way, they cut me all up through the middle. After that I was class B, I wasn't really fit, and they sent me to Maidenhead, to a big holding camp there. It was just outside the range of what they called the war zone in Great Britain. My wife, Daisy, came up to see me. Our little boy Kenny stayed with aunts but Daisy brought little Jean, my daughter, up to see me.

"Because I was re-classed down, I lost my rank, and I was transferred out of the Wilts into the Service Corps. The funny thing was when I was in the Service Corps they regraded me B class and were going to send me for convalescence up in Scotland. There were too many air raids in London. Instead of doing that they sent me up to Scotland and made up a formation of B class soldiers for active service. I ended up out in Egypt! I was there for 15 months. I finished up in the Ordnance Corps.

"We went to Egypt by boat. We slept in hammocks. Well, we slept in our coats until we got to the Med, to Alexandria. We were kitted out and had a day's run into Cairo. We ended up under canvas in the bloody desert. That was just after Christmas 1941. I got an office job. I was a clerk class one. In Cairo was the Reme headquarters for the Middle East. I used to go down to the Reme offices. An officer I knew there said to me 'By the way I've got some information for you.' I said 'What's that, sir?' He said 'Anyone in His Majesty's Forces that comes out in the first 16 classes and has a military installation near his home is guaranteed a job there.' When the Second World War finished they were bringing men out in classes, one to 12. I was class 9, so I came out in August 1945.

"I came home and I had to register as a civilian at a place up Boreham Road. Then I had to go to the dole office which by then was down at Silver Street near

**The Territorials at Weymouth Camp in August 1928.
Len Ingram is standing second from right.**

**Beckford Hospital, at Gipsy Lane, during the 1950s.**

the Ship & Punch Bowl pub. The fellow there said 'Here you are, go up to the Reme Workshops.' I went up there. The first person I saw was Dick Webber. I said 'You know me, don't you.' He said 'Vaguely.' I said 'You ought to, I'm a Warminster man.' He said 'We can give you a storeman's class B job.' I said 'That will do, I don't mind.' My first wage up there was £4 12s.

"When I came out of the Army I had a letter from Dorset County Council asking me if I wanted my old job back at Beckford Lodge. They were looking after the wounded up there. I went up and saw the matron. I said 'I've been away six years and I'm being offered only a pound extra to what I had before. That's no good to me.' I was glad I didn't take it. I was wise to go to the Reme. When the National Health Service came in it put paid to anything I would have got at Beckford. That wouldn't have been no good to me.

"When I came out of the Army I got a gratuity of £87, and I had £47 from the hospital. The hospital didn't pay me the full sum because I didn't stop on with them. That was a terrific lot of money. The wife and I decided to get a bit of furniture for our home. I said 'Come on mother, let's go and see about a suite of furniture.' We had got some bits and pieces before off Davis who had a shop at the High Street. We went in. The first thing he said to me was 'I don't give credit.' I walked out. He followed me on to the pavement outside. He said 'Oh, Mr Ingram.' I said 'No, you don't. I didn't ask for credit.' That's because I was working class. If I had been anybody else, say someone important, he would have allowed me to settle up at the end of the month. I didn't want credit in any case. That shook me. I had just come out of the Army and I was willing to spend 40 quid. I had been in the Army abroad, fighting for my country, while he was running that shop in Warminster. He'd probably been making money hand over fist out of the military in Warminster. The wife and I went on up

**Staff at the Castle Steam Laundry, George Street, in the early 1920s.
The laundry took its name from its location in the yard of the former Castle Inn.**

to the Co-op and saw Mr Turner there. He gave us ten shillings, our train fare to Bristol, and sent us down to the Co-op there. He phoned them up and told them we were coming. We bought our furniture there and we got what we wanted for just under £37. They delivered it. That was some kitchen chairs, a kitchen table and two armchairs.

"At the Reme I joined the scheme where I paid 2s 6d a month in and they put so much in, to ensure I got gratuity. At the Reme I went from class B to class A storeman. I'll tell you what. When I got up the Reme I could see there were men there that should have been in the Army. There were chaps there that went into bolt-holes and stayed as civilians. They might have done home guard duty but they crept into the clerical side of the War. They might have been doing clerical stuff but they didn't know so much as me and I was in the Army. Well, when I first went up the Reme there was Yanks in there. They cleared out and the military came in from Tidworth. They re-organised the place at Longleat, they re-organised the place at Westbury, and the overlap came to Warminster. Some of them were in a classification higher than myself. I had just been made up again. Those that were below the line had to drop back to being labourers which was a pound or 30 bob a week less. That was a big difference if you had a wife and family.

"I was doing alright. I put money from the Army in a Post Office account. I had a nice little bank balance of £40 or £50 to fall back on. That was a lot. I'm telling you. When I was a boy you could nearly have bought a house with that. A post came up for foreman in the yard, at the Reme, looking after all the labour. To do that meant I had to come down a class but I had a strong trade union who said 'They can't bring you down, don't let them say you're not as they think you should be.' Having done my six years in the Army I had a background whereby the military would look after me. The job was supervising the civilians, both male and female, doing certain things.

"They had a library up the Reme. I went up and saw the chap. I said 'Have you got any books on administration of civilians in Reme?' He said 'Oh Christ, I've got one somewhere.' Nobody had ever asked for it before. He said 'Come back tomorrow.' I went back. He said 'I've found it.' I said 'Jolly good. Is it alright if I take it home?' He said 'Yes, as long as you sign for it.' It was the sort of book an officer would read. The wife said 'What's all that?' I said 'I've put in for another job. I'm reading up. I hope I get it.'

"They had a board and six of us went before this board. There were two military chaps and four civilians. I went in. There was a major. He was the chairman of the board. I had contacted him about different things before but there was no familiarity between us. He asked me a lot of questions. They all asked me questions. I asked them questions. They said 'Where did you get the questionnaire to know what to ask us?' The major said 'He has drawn a book from the library to brush up his knowledge of the job.' That impressed them. I was the only one of the six who applied who had taken the trouble to find out what the job was all about. Of course I got the job.

"There was uproar about it. Someone called in the Union. The others disliked me because I was local and ex-Army. They thought it was all planned but it wasn't. The officers in charge called me in. They were re-organising Reme. They said 'You've got the job, and you've got to go through the yard with a fine tooth comb.' I checked all the ladies and all the men, found out what was right and wrong, I checked out what was happening with the police at the gate. I had to do my job and I know it upset a lot of people. The police were alright because they had set duties but I changed everyone else. They'd been going along in their own smooth way but it wasn't Army like. I had that Army experience. I had to be strict. The women sweeping

**The view across Wilson Square and the Reme Workshops, 1986.**

and cleaning offices were on semi-skilled pay. They had their pay plus ten shillings a week. When the new colonel came in he went through the background of all the civilians on the staff. He said to me 'You're going to lose some of your labour. Your ladies are going to have their payments stopped.'

"The word came out of the office to the union people. I was a trade unionist on the employees' side but I was still a trade unionist on the management side. A trade unionist chap said to me 'You're not going to stop my women having their money.' I said 'I'm not stopping your women's money. I've got to carry out orders that the money be cut to a labourer's pay.' Ten shillings a week knocked off a woman's wage in them days was terrible. It happened. My staff was cut, the police staff was cut, they all had to come down to something they didn't want to do. They were locked in the old ways, what they were used to, and then the new colonel came and said what had to be done. I had to carry it out.

"They tried somewhere along the line to cut my grade down from two to three. As it happened I got upgraded before I retired so I made a bigger pension and a bigger hand out. I came out on the highest pay for that grade when I retired. I did that job as foreman from 1961 to 1973. I got the Imperial Service Medal. All together I had 30 years in Reme. I only left through ill-health. I retired four months before my 65th birthday because I had water trouble. I finished Christmas '73. My time was happy at the Reme. I made a lot of friends and I made a lot of enemies.

"After the Second World War I stood as a Labour candidate at an election. There was a Labour government in after the War. They revived the Labour Party in Warminster after the War and I got mixed in with Tom Davies who worked up at the Barley Research Station at Boreham Road. He's dead and gone now. He and his wife were very big labour people. There was another chap from up Bell Hill. He worked at Bell Potteries. His name was George Scourfield. We had all come out of the services. Turner, who had come down from London and worked for the RE's on the buildings, was another Labour man. He was Chairman of the Council once. They persuaded me to stand for Labour but of course I didn't get nowhere. It was all bankers and high-ups about here. That was about 1947. Trouble was, the Labour movement didn't spread all over the country like they thought it would. Rationing and all that carried on into the 1950s and the people voted Labour out of office. Things didn't work out. I gave up active interest in politics.

"Before the Second World War, when my son Kenny was small, when I was in the Territorials, me and the wife used to go dancing. We loved dancing. We were dancers. After I finished with the Labour thing and gave up politics, the wife and I used to listen to the old time dancing on the wireless This is before telly mind. *Time For Old Time* was the name of the wireless programme. This is about 1948. They had dances in Warminster. Mr Vincent used to run old time dances at the Drill Hall at Imber Road. Bill Hext, who worked in Coates and Parker's, he used to be in Lucas and Foot's, the paper shop, he used to run the dances at the Old Bell. Up the back.

"My daughter Jean was only young, about 16, she said she was going up to see about the dancing. In the meantime our son Kenny was working on the railway. I claimed him and got him a job at the Reme. He was there a couple of years and he was called up on National Service. He had to do two years. He went to Germany and he was in the band, played the flute and one thing and another. He was demobbed. He came home on the day that me, the wife, and the daughter, went up to the Town Hall to see the old time dancing. George Wright was there. Percy Vincent and his wife were there. That was 1948. They said 'You've got to come next week.' We went up and stood by the door. 'Come on in.' they said. 'Dance.' The wife tried to get me on this old time dancing.

"The Mother's Union and the different women's organisations used to run dances. We started going and we started dancing. Some top people from Frome started coming to Warminster to dance. A good atmosphere built up. They liked us. They said to us come early to the dos and we'll teach you how to dance properly. They were professionals. That's how we got into the dancing world. Different people and different bands would come along. We started to go to other places like Westbury. Me, the wife, Jean, and my other son Bobby were going out to these dances and having a good time. This was the 1950s.

"Unfortunately we lost Bobby. He had kidney trouble and died. That was the time when they had no what's it, dialysis, for kidney sufferers. He was taken ill. When they diagnosed him at Bath they wanted to take one of his kidneys away but the bad one had damaged the good kidney. There was no hope. Within six weeks he was gone. Of course that shattered us. He went dancing with us, he was only a young man, a boy really.

"Anyhow, to console ourselves, we carried on with the dancing and got involved with big things. We went to Blackpool, Weston Super Mare, and Southampton, all they places, dancing and mixing with the top people in the old time dancing world. I danced with the top ladies. They were in the television world. I've got photographs and all of it. We gave up dancing five years ago because of the wife's health, her legs went, and I had water trouble. I had to keep going out to pass water.

"We met people from all over the place. Mr Hext gave up, Mr and Mrs Curtis took over the club. The wife and I were joint leaders of the Warminster Old Time Dance Club at one time. It used to be called the Gay Nineties Old Time Dance Club. The club continued with different people, it went down a bit but came up again. After I had an operation for water I had a heart attack, then I got gout, then two years ago I got shingles. I think when you stop doing something your body starts going down. We'd been going out three or four nights a week dancing. We'd been going to Salisbury, Devizes, Bradford on Avon, and Bath. In the old time dance world you were never called by your christian names. It was never 'Here's Len and Daisy.' It was always 'Here comes the Ingrams' and 'Here comes the Browns.' They always talked in senior tones. It was never 'Here comes Harry Brown.' Oh, they were wonderful times. We've had a wonderful life, no doubt about it.

"Warminster is terrible today. Why? When a person is taught in an era of discipline, nice talking, and you learned manners in school, you were kept away from viciousness. Like we used to play football as kids up the rec, it was rough and tumble but it was a game of life. Kids used to fight among themselves but there was harmony. But now there seems to be, well, there's two camps.

"Warminster only had a population of 4,000. Everybody knew everybody to the extent that when we were young boys if we went from Pound Street where I lived to say, Bishopstrow or Boreham, someone would say 'Hey, you don't belong here, get out.' Every neighbourhood knew its neighbourhood. You were recognised as a stranger. If anybody from St John's School, or somewhere, came up to our playing field

**Daisy and Len Ingram at the Carnival Old Time Ball at the Old Bell Hotel on 13 September 1969.**

at Pound Street we'd say 'We know where you come from.' Everybody knew everybody else and where they lived. Everybody knew everybody else's place too.

"Today we're so cosmopolitan, you get people come in and they quote things they know nothing about. I was listening to someone, a couple, the other week. They had sold their business up in London for about £90,000 and come to Warminster and bought a house for £70,000. These people come into Warminster but they don't belong. People like that use Warminster for themselves.

"When we were doing the old time dancing I used to like a joke. I was talking with a chap, one of these high-ups that came to Warminster, and he had money. He said to me 'Are you a Warminster man?' I said 'Oh yes.' For a joke I said to him 'You've got to have a certificate to be a Warminsterite.' He said 'Do you?' I said 'Yes, when you've been here about 25 years you can get a certificate from the Town Council.' At that point he realised I was winding him up. He didn't half choke me off. He was as mad as anything. I didn't care. He deserved it. He was one of those people who had been here five minutes, well, ten years perhaps, and thought he knew it all.

"I heard another chap one day talking about Warminster in the old days. I said 'How long have you lived here?' He said 'About ten years. I came from London.' I said 'The things you're talking about you must have read in Warminster history books. You must have got a book out of the Library because you don't know nothing about what went on in Warminster years ago.' He couldn't of.

"When I was a young man I and Nelson Gay would cycle to Frome to go to pictures on Saturday night. We'd go two on a bike. One on the saddle and one pedalling. Half way you'd change over. You had to be careful when you got to Frome because they knew you were strangers. Same as if you went to Westbury and Trowbridge. Each village, each suburb of every town, was a community on its own. Today there's so many strangers, I suppose it's wrong to say it, but they don't belong. You and I belong because we were born here, we're part and parcel of the town's development but these people from London that come in, they're not Warminster and they never will be.

"Warminster has gone wrong. The Council were building houses for ordinary Warminster people. Then someone high-up said 'You've got to stop building Council houses. From now on you must allow others to build houses which can be sold.' The result is people building houses to fill their pockets. Land is being developed by speculators. The people who build the houses then disappear with the money and leave expensive eyesores behind them. This extra development puts pressures on the sewers and other facilities, so the rates go up, and we, the locals, in Council houses get penalised. We end up having to pay more in rates.

"Our rents and rates have gone up. It's the times, you can't alter the times. There's all these houses being built in Warminster and look at the price of them. These developers have got to keep in competition with what's happening elsewhere in London and the South East. You can blame the Council, you can blame the government for telling the Council not to build any more houses. Now Warminster is surrounded with bloody houses that the likes of us can't afford to buy.

"I don't like the policies of the present Government, the Conservatives. Well it's not the policies of all the Conservatives, it's the policy of Mrs Thatcher and the one or two around her that have to agree with her. Her policy is, you can read it in the paper, a person with more than

**The river Wylye at Smallbrook, 1986.**

£6,000 must look after themselves. That's wrong. Why, if you have been careful and saved yourself some money, tried to help yourself, why oh why should you be penalised? In a way I'm satisfied that I have nothing to do with the authorities because today, when the pensions go up and some of these people have rent and rates rebates, as soon as these people get extra money the Council takes it away from them. They're marking time but they've still got to buy things that are dearer than the week before. I know someone with an invalid husband and they are getting a £2.50 rent rebate. On the 1st April this year it finished, the rebate book had to go back. Now they've got to find that £2.50. Well, £5 really, because their rent has gone up £2.50. They've had a rise on their pension but it's only half of the extra what they've got to pay out.

"Years ago there was no such thing as a mugging. You could walk around Warminster as safe as anything. There were hardly any lights and the police force was small. If you did do anything you were known, the community was that small. I remember, as a boy, once going down the Common and an old lady said to me 'Hello, you're so and so, aren't you?' You didn't dare ask the question 'How do you know?' You had to respect your elders. You were known. Mugging is a modern word. There was no big crime, I can't remember nothing like that. Today the prisons are full, so those who do mugging have to go and dig the victim's garden. It's ridiculous. It's not punishment to them, it's just a nuisance because it stops them going to football or something like that. That's all.

"I remember an old chap named Mr Joyce who had a photographer's shop in Silver Street. When he used to take a photograph of a small group he'd have the camera on a tripod and he'd hold up glass things. Four boys got into Joyce's and stole those glass things. They weren't quite sure who told the police but those boys sold what they had pinched for sixpence each to some other boys. The police knew who had these plates and caught them. They were had up in the Town Hall. Two of the boys were birched and one went to the Reformatory. The case was open, closed and shut. All that has been taken away now. Do-gooders in society, people working for the DHSS, so-called doing good have put paid to that.

"But look at these little kiddies that have died through their father being bamboozled. Someone thinks they've seen the baby getting hit about but the DHSS don't act until it's too late. Afterwards they find the kiddie dead or beat to pieces. It's crazy. Years ago the

**The front of the Dene, 1986.**

community was so small someone would get wind of anybody stepping out of line straight away and they'd be caught and punished. No messing.

"You used to get fined five shillings if you were caught riding a bike at night without a light. Squire Temple, the magistrate, used to ride a big bike to court. He had a big Sunbeam bike with a double bar on it. He hated motorists. If any motorist came before the Bench when he was on it at the Town Hall, he'd be fined between one and five guineas. That were a lot of money. When I was on the dole in the 1930s I used to go into the gallery in the Town Hall on court days and listen to some of the cases. The Clerk of the court would advise and Temple would make a judgement. He hated cars, he said they were a stinking noise and a nuisance. He was against cars or any progress with cars, he favoured bicycles.

"When I was a boy, George Street had two gas lights one side of the road, one lamp the other, the road was grit and there were no markings and it was a residential area. It was all clean. The Council men used to keep places clean. Not today, there's filth and litter everywhere. You get letters in the *Warminster Journal* written by gentlemen, we've got to call them that, saying so and so should be done. That's newcomers writing those letters. They're not part and parcel of the community so they do nothing about it themselves. A Colonel somebody said 'Why don't people get off their bottoms and pick up the litter?' Why doesn't he get off his bottom? I see the school children were sent out to pick up the rubbish but they weren't given no gloves to do it. That's wrong. And they only did a certain place, they didn't come down here.

"Each generation has got 20 years between it. Every 15 years it changes. I was brought up on my grandparents' Victorian values, when you had to be decent. Then, the next era, something else will change, like a war comes along. The Great War altered things and the next War. Nobody wants to go back to the days when if you didn't have a job you didn't have no money like I went through. Today, there's a lot of people dwelling on what they can get for nothing. These helpers on the DHSS get people stuff out of the ordinary. Years ago we would have called that a fiddle. Sort of like 'I'll get that for you, don't worry.' I think there's a great danger at the moment where young girls can have a baby, they ain't married and the DHSS gets them a Council house. They don't pay no rent and the DHSS looks after them. Yet, a widow gets her money cut down. It's wrong. It's not fair.

"I worked out how much I have paid out in council house rent since 1936. One of my grandsons helped me work it out. It came to about £7,000. The rent went up in leaps and bounds, when we first came in here, at this house at the Dene, in 1958, it was £1 and ninepence a week all in. Look at it now. It's £59 a fortnight now. That's all out of proportion now.

"There's people that can get the DHSS to pay their rent to the Council. After five years they can buy their house at a reduced rate. They get the benefit of that, but all the time the DHSS has been paying the rent, those people have done nothing for the community, they've paid nothing for the services they've had.

"Looking back, we knew some good old days, well, they were funny days, odd days. The stock question I'm asked by young people today is 'Why were things like that, why was it?' I say to them 'Why is today like it is with all this cruelty, and why is the country in such a state today?' You can't explain why. When you explain how we lived to the younger generation they won't believe it or they can't understand it. Oh well."

# LIFE WITH THE ARTINDALES
## Marjorie Yeates
*11 May 1988*

"My name is Marjorie Yeates. I was born at Westbury on 21st September 1907. My father was Arthur Henry Meaden and he worked in the mines in Wales for a time but later he worked at the Westbury Iron Works. I don't know much about his family. He might have been born at Westbury. He had a sister living there. My mother's name before she married was Ellen Mason.

"I was one of 14 children but when we lived at Westbury there were just four of us children at home. The older ones had grown up and gone out into the world. My mother referred to the four of us as her 'second' family. That was two boys and two girls - Fred and Jack, Lena and myself. Lena was the youngest. We were still going to school.

"Our elder brother Tom was in the Navy. The others were all girls. My favourite sister married an Australian in the First World War and she emigrated to Australia when she was 19. She died, unfortunately, due to a mistake. She had an operation and the doctor left a medical instrument inside her. It killed her. He was an English doctor that did that. I think he was hounded out of Australia after that but whether he came back to this country I don't know.

"That sister had four sons and a daughter. The girl was named after me. She came over to England about ten or eleven years ago. She wanted to see her mother's family because none of them had seen us over here. She stayed with my husband and me at Weymouth for seven weeks. She's deaf and dumb. I had to write a letter to the authorities to say that I would have her and look after her. I got very worried. I didn't know how I was going to cope with her. We went to the Citizens' Advice Bureau. They advised us to get in touch with a hard-of-hearing organisation. The president or whoever he was, of that, came to see us. He was really marvellous. They went up to Waterloo and fetched her and they took her back to Waterloo when it was time for her to go. They even took her to the Isle Of Wight for a day. They were really wonderful. She's never forgot it. We still correspond. We've got a friend in Weymouth who has got relatives living near her in Australia.

"One of my sisters went to Canada. She got killed in Canada. She had no family. Jack did his time in the Navy. He married an English girl but she was born in Africa. He brought her back here once. Jack died in Africa; he's buried in Cape Town. Brother Tom died in Ireland. Although we were a big family we all scattered. We were no good to one another. We didn't even correspond. I've got a sister in Bath, she's 92; and one in Calne, she's 94. And there's me. There's just us three left now out of the lot.

"My family were living at Heywood, near Westbury, when the First World War broke out. Father insisted on going off to war. He put his age back to go. It got granny Meaden down. She was on the verge of a nervous breakdown. The doctor said that she had to get away from Heywood. So, we went from Heywood to stay with my aunt Lou at the Furlong in Warminster. I can't remember how long we stayed with aunt Lou but the doctor said we were overcrowded. There was Fred and Jack, Lena and myself, besides Lou and her family. The doctor got us a house at West Street, Warminster.

"The house at West Street was near to Captain Taylor's house. There was a row of derelict houses between Captain Taylor's and our house. They were knocked down and a single house built there. Fred and Rose Baker lived in there. Father used to stack all his wood in those old cottages. Lower down, my sister Lena and I used to play 'mothers and fathers' in one of them. We had tea parties in there. We also went out into the fields at the back and made daisy chains. We never had any toys to play with.

"I remember once when the snow was on the ground. There used to be a woman come in regularly from Corsley with a pony and trap, shopping. She was coming down West Street one day and Jack chucked a snowball at her. It hit the horse. She got off the cart and reckoned she was going to get hold of Jack. He ran indoors and got in the lavatory. He said 'Don't let her find me.' The woman knocked at the front door and said she wanted a word with him. I said 'He isn't here.' I told a lie. Jack got away with it. The woman was upset because the snowball had hit the horse and made it jump.

"Jack was a devil. He really was. We could never get him in at night. He always wanted to stop out playing. My parents tried everything. One night mother told him she was going to ask the police to get him in. He got under mother's cloak to hide because he thought the police were coming. He was a bounder. He and I were bad friends.

"Jack and Fred went to the Close School, under Mr Dewey. Jack, the devil that he was, got into trouble one day at school. He chucked the ink pot at old Dewey. He had the cane for that and he also had his name put in the log book. He disgraced us.

"I went to the Minster School, at Vicarage Street, when we came to Warminster. I liked it there but I never learnt much. I was a proper idiot. I didn't like arithmetic. When it was hot we used to go out into the playground and have our lessons under a big tree. Miss Ludgate was the governess. The other teacher boarded with Miss Ludgate. And Miss Ludgate's father, Mr Ludgate, lived there too. He used to go out every morning for a walk. He'd go up Ash Walk and take a dry crust of bread, always. He'd eat that while sitting on the seat up there.

"My pals at the Minster School included Eva Miles, Dolly Reynolds and Kitty Sawyer. Kitty lived at West Street. Her father worked at the Brewery and he hung himself. I don't know why he committed suicide. Kitty found him. She was still a youngster at school then. She went away to her sister at Portsmouth for a time to get over the shock. We were all told at school that we were not to say anything about it to her when she came back. She had a huge white patch of hair. Her hair, a round patch of it, went white with the shock. She eventually got over it.

"We used to have to go to church on Sundays after going to Sunday School first. We went to the Minster Church. There was a man called Robert Hill who lived in the shop near Charlton's at West Street. He used to go to church every Sunday morning and we used to sit in his row. He used to bring a bag of sweets to church and he'd give us all a sweet to eat in church. We looked forward to that.

"I left the Minster School when I was 14. I've still got my school-leaving paper. My education definitely wasn't sufficient. My parents didn't tell me anything when I was growing up. I had to learn for myself. We never had any books in home.

"After I left school I went to work as a

daily help to my old governess Miss Ludgate. She lived in the house at the top of Sambourne Road, the one that used to be the Boot pub [now No.60]. The man [Brian Davis] who works in Warminster Library lives there now. Working for Miss Ludgate was the first job I had.

"I was 14, just left school, when I met Harold Yeates, who is now my husband. We were childhood sweethearts. He was a Warminster boy. He was born at West Street. He was a friend of my brother's and they both used to keep pigeons. Harold used to come to my house at West Street. I used to have a flutter every time I saw him. He was also the Sunday paper boy and he delivered to us. My mother knew that I was sweet on him and she and father wouldn't let me go to the door to take the Sunday paper. Still, we struck up a friendship. My mother did her utmost to part us.

"Harold and I did all our courting in Warminster. You know Copheap Lane? There's a seat half way up there. We used to sit on there cuddling. It didn't matter if it was frosty or bitter cold. We used to wait to hear the St Laurence's clock strike, then we used to go home. We often went to that seat at Copheap Lane. I enjoyed my courting days. They were marvellous times. They were great fun.

"Most of our courting was done, secretly, out in the woods. I had a friend, Chris Acland, she's dead now, and I had to take her with me as an alibi. My mother would say 'You've been out with Yeates.' I'd say 'No, I've been with Chris Acland.' If Harold and I went to the pictures we daren't sit together. If we went to church we had to sit one behind the other. One Sunday, my mother hid behind the tombstones in the churchyard, waiting to see us come out of church together. Her efforts were all to no avail.

"I left Miss Ludgate's and then worked as a daily for Mrs Verity. She used to be at the Reformatory School at Tascroft. After her husband died she went to live with her mother over Payne's bakery in George Street. Mrs Verity moved to Bristol, to a guest house, and she asked my mother if I could go with her. My mother was delighted, to get me away from Harold Yeates. I went to Bristol and I was paid about half-a-crown a week. Harold came down to Bristol to see me one day and he missed his train back. There was a woman, a daily, working for Mrs Verity, and I took Harold to her place at Bedminster. She put him up for the night. He got up the next morning and got the milk train. He worked at Bush & Co's, the house furnishers, in Warminster. Luckily he got back to work in time.

"I got fed up at Bristol. I got up early one morning, walked to the station and got the train home. Mrs Verity wrote to my mother. She sent my insurance cards and that. She said in her letter that she thought I had left on account of a boy. She was right. I wanted to be closer to Harold.

"My next job was as a cook at the Manor House in Bratton. I more or less learnt to cook there. Two of my sisters, Nell and Molly, had worked there as cooks before me. That's how I came to get the job. Nell was there first, then Molly, and I was the third one to go there. Once a month I had a weekend, well, it was a night really, off. Harold used to cycle back with me in the morning before he went to work.

"After a while I changed jobs. I left the Manor House at Bratton and got a job as a daily, doing housework and cleaning, at Chambers' shop in Warminster Market Place. Mr Chambers was a jeweller and watch-repairer. I was only a daily there, I didn't sleep in. The Chambers' had a son and a daughter. They were prim and proper, as most shop people were in those days.

**Mr Artindale and Nurse Crowle, at East House, about 1932.**

"I wasn't at Chambers' long before I saw a job advertised as a cook at East House, off East Street, Warminster. That was Mr and Mrs Artindale's. I went up and tried for it. I had a reference from Chambers'. I had to have one to start at Artindale's. I didn't see Mr and Mrs Artindale when I applied. Nurse Crowle interviewed me. She was the boss of the show. She was the housekeeper. She was an old fossil. Anyhow, I got the job as cook at Artindale's. I was terribly young to do that but they were desperate to get somebody. I could do it though because I had been doing similar work at Bratton.

"I started as the cook at Mr Artindale's about 1923. Kitty Sawyer, who I had been at the Minster School with, was the parlourmaid there. I met up with her again after having lost touch with her. Kitty's brother, Bob Sawyer, also worked at East House, as the odd job boy. There were two gardeners, Mr Rudman and Mr Prince. Rudman was the kitchen gardener and Prince saw to the greenhouses and the flowers. Joey Crofts helped in the gardens and was also the chauffeur. Joey's wife drowned herself down Smallbrook. I don't know why she did it. Joey Crofts married again. He'd been working at East House a long time. He lived in one of the cottages.

"Rudman lived in the other cottage. Rudman died after I left. I've got a cutting about his funeral. It reads 'The funeral of the late Mr Henry Rudman, of East House Cottage, Warminster, whose death we reported last week, took place at South Wraxall, Bradford On Avon, on Saturday, the Rev H.M. Bennett officiating. The chief mourners were: Mr and Mrs W. Norris (son-in-law and daughter); Miss M. Norris (granddaughter); Mrs C. Huntley (niece); Mrs Shoemark (niece); Mr and Mrs R. Mortimer (nephew and niece); Mr W. Mortimer (nephew). Among those also present at the church were: Mrs Artindale (East House, Warminster); Miss K.

**The rear of East House, about 1930.**

Sawyer, Mr W. Kitley, Mr T. Northeast, Mr J. Crofts, and Mr G. Prince, of Warminster; Mr J. Godolphin (Bradford Leigh); and others.'

"The East End Avenue housing estate is built on Artindale's old gardens. The front of Rudman's house led into Roly Poly Path. Crofts' was over the other side of the yard where the cars went up. There was a double garage for the two cars. They were beautiful cars, I'll tell you about them in a minute. Crofts regularly washed them. There was a well outside, at the back of Rudman's house. They must have filled that in. There was like a big shed, a barn, there too, with lofts where they used to put the apples. They had racks up very high.

"Everyday Rudman used to come down to me. He used to call me 'Miss Marjey'. He used to say 'Now what do you want today Miss Marjey?' He brought fruit or vegetables, whatever I asked for. If he had anything special that he had grown he'd bring that down. He didn't go over the top, he wasn't flush. He knew what he had and how to eke things out. Like he'd bring so many strawberries for the dining room or whatever.

"I was in the kitchen most of the time. I was cooking. There were no mod-cons. It was an old-fashioned house with nothing modern in it. There was no such thing as fridges. You must be joking. We never even had an icebox. Nothing at all. I had a range with double ovens. To get the water hot we had a round stove that burnt coke. I had to get up early to see to that, otherwise we'd have no hot water for the day. There were two big tables in the kitchen. We had a white deal one for preparing the food on and a bit farther over a polished one where we maids used to have our meals. Beyond that was a horrible scullery. It had a great big old sink and a knife machine to clean the knives. It was a stone sink and it was horrible. The buckets of coal were kept out there in the scullery. Bob Sawyer used to get the coal in. He was a good chap. Our routine was hard work.

"As well as cooking I had to help with other things in the house. We had to get the rooms to a certain temperature. Crowle saw that Mr Artindale's room and the bathroom were a certain temperature in the morning. It was open fires. He wouldn't come down unless the temperature was right. I had to light the fire and I had to clean it. I also had to clean the front door. That's all the cleaning I done.

"Us girls had our bedrooms right at the top of the house. There was a bell. Outside the Mrs' bedroom was a staircase going up to our bedrooms. In fact there were two ways of going up. There was the main staircase and the kitchen staircase. If we weren't up, Mrs used to pull the bell. We used to oversleep. She'd pull on the bell to get us up. If we were late Mr Artindale's water wouldn't be hot.

"He used to get up for breakfast. He had a little single bed in this great big bedroom. He used to wear a hat with a tassel on it. It was a white hat with a long tassel. Crowle used to go and tuck him in bed at night. She really nursed him. He thought the world of her. Crowle was Artindale's nurse and she went everywhere and did everything for him. If he only wanted to go out in the garden for a walk she used to take him. She always used to say that she took a bath in cold stone water, freezing water, everyday, even if it was a cold frosty morning. Then she used to go for a run around the garden. She used to say she did that but I don't believe it. I don't believe it was freezing cold water.

**The front of East House, about 1930.**

"Nurse Crowle lived in at Artindale's but later lived with her sister, next to Butcher's bakery and shop, at Silver Street. She had every Sunday off and went to her sister's for lunch. She used to come back to Artindale's at six o'clock, on the dot, every Sunday evening. That would allow which ever of us girls was in to go out for a couple of hours after dinner. One day she'd gone out to her sister and I was in. Mrs Artindale came into the kitchen and said 'You needn't wait for nurse to come in, Marjorie, you can go.' So I went out. When nurse came back and found that I had gone without her permission to let me go there was trouble. She had something to say about it and Mrs. Artindale sacked her. She had the sack. Mr Artindale never really liked me after that. It wasn't my fault. Missus had a right to tell me I could go. That was the end of Nurse Crowle. That was quite a while after I started there.

"Mr and Mrs Artindale were an odd couple. He was 30 years older than her. He was a gentleman, he had means, and he had made his money in China. He went out to China when she was baby. Somehow he knew her parents and he told them that when he returned from China he would marry her. And he did. That was before I started working for them. He didn't marry her for her money but she might have married him for his!

"I don't know what he did out in China. Once a year a large chest of China tea was delivered to East House. The Artindales never drank any other sort of tea, it was always real China tea. That tea was beautifully packed in the chest. We had to take it out and put it into big tin tea caddies when it came. Mr Artindale always used to like a slice of lemon in his cup of tea. Lemon China tea. For all I know he could have made his money with a tea plantation out in China.

"Before they came to Warminster, Mr and Mrs Artindale lived at Fisherton Delamere in the Wylye Valley. They had a much bigger staff in those days. She told me. She said she used to have her very own lady's maid to help her dress in the mornings. She led the life of a lady. She told me once how she used to do a lot of horse-riding out there.

"On one occasion Mrs Artindale got pregnant. She was going to have a baby but she insisted on going horse-riding. I don't know if she fell off the horse or what but she lost the baby and that was that.

"Mr Artindale was originally from Lancashire but he didn't have a northern accent. He had lost that. He was a proper gentleman. He was familiar with the staff. He was very nice. He called me by my first name. I had to call him 'sir'. He never raised his voice to you and I never ever heard him swear. He was a good living man. He didn't smoke. He wasn't a great drinker neither, but he always had a whisky and soda after his dinner.

"He was the first President of the Warminster Flying Club. He had a pigeon loft up at East House. Joey Crofts used to take the pigeons out on race days. There were cups and trophies on display in East House.

"At one time Mr Artindale was a Justice of the Peace in Warminster but that was before I started working for him. When I was in his employ he very rarely went into town. He used to go to church at St. John's, on the Boreham Road, every Sunday. He was a sidesman or a vicar's warden there. He never tried to push his religion on to you. He left £1,000 to St John's in his will. He's buried at St. John's.

"He was fairly short, but not fat, and he had a moustache. He was always smartly dressed. Nurse Crowle used to see to that. Very often he used to wear plus fours. He had a rabbit warren up on the downs, near Imber. He had a gamekeeper, Mr Wright, who lived up Imber way, at Ladywell. Mr Wright's son, Bernie, used to help out too. I remember once Wright caught a poacher up on the warren and he brought him down to East House for Mr Artindale to deal with.

"Mr and Mrs Artindale would invite their friends during the autumn for a shooting party. Joey Crofts and some other men would go up and put wire-netting all round the warren so that the rabbits couldn't escape. When it was all fenced in the party would go up and shoot the rabbits. I had to make up a big hamper of food for the guns to take up on the warren. They'd come back to the house for a dinner at night, chauffeurs and all.

"They brought the catch, the bag, back. They'd bring down a sackful of rabbits and I had to skin them all and cook them. The dogs had the meat but the men had the soup. They only had soup out of the rabbits. Mr Artindale always used to give the elderly people in the Furlong a rabbit each and when he was fishing I had to clean and take them fish. At Christmas he saw that they all had a hundredweight of coal as a present. He was generous like that.

"There was a lot of game brought back from the warren because Mr Artindale and his friends also shot birds. They shot loads of partridges. I had to clean them. I got used to it. I'd never had game to do before. I'd never drawn a chicken. Nothing like that.

"They used to have quail. This used to make me sick. They'd have quail on bits of toast. They're a small bird and they were served whole, and never drawn. They were cooked without having their inside taken out. They went to the dining room table like that. When the plates came back, it was sickening, because there would be all the insides left all over the plates. I didn't like to see that.

"They used to have a lot of jugged hare and that had to be very high. They were not paunched like rabbit. They'd come down as they were. They were absolutely crawling. I've had maggots all up my arm when I was jugging hares. Jugged hare is really delicious. I loved that. Artindales loved them. And nice high pheasants. I used to sneak one out of the house. My boyfriend, Harold, would come up, to take me out. He'd arrive just as the pheasant was coming back from the dinner table and I could get some of that. It stunk. It was so high.

"They never ate anything unless it was really high. The game was kept down in the cellar below the house and it would be crawling with maggots. It was rancid with maggots. One day we had a big piece of venison down the cellar. I had to go down there for some reason and I could see that this venison was covered with maggots. It was absolutely moving. I said to Mrs Artindale, madam, that I thought the venison ought to be cooked. 'Oh no,' she said, 'It's not high enough yet.'

"Mr Artindale had a gun room in the house. It was on the ground floor, just off the hall. The guns were kept in cases. He used to sit in there nearly all day. He'd spend hours in there but I never ever saw him cleaning the guns. He'd just be sat there. He used to read a lot. He had books in the house.

"He used to go fishing as well. He used to go to Wylye to fish. I remember he went fishing one election time. Joey Crofts, the chauffeur, had taken him out. Mr Artindale was out fishing and Mrs Artindale heard the election results on the wireless or something. She said 'Come on girls, we must go and let Mr Artindale know the result.' She always referred to me and Kitty as girls, she never called us the maids.

"Mr Artindale had two cars, a Humber and a Rolls-Royce. He bought the Rolls-Royce for her. She used to drive. It was a light creamy one. He had a deep maroon Humber. She couldn't wait for him to come home from fishing. She liked a drink. She was sozzled. Kit and I went with her in the Rolls-Royce. We sat in the back. Instead of us going to where Mr Artindale was fishing, she took a wrong turning and I don't know where we went. It seemed like we went all round the world. I think we headed Shaftesbury way. Eventually, a terrific thunderstorm broke. She was going up a little narrow country lane and she got the Rolls stuck at an angle in a ditch. You couldn't go one way or the other. It was facing into the hedge. She didn't seem particularly worried. We had just passed a farm. She said 'Come on girls, we'll have to walk back to the farm and get the farmer.' It was about five o'clock. The men were just leaving work. Three or four farmworkers came to help get the car out of the ditch. They got us out. She gave every one of those a pound each. That was a lot of money in those days. After they got the car out we came on home. Mr Artindale was already home. He was annoyed because he was worried where she was. The car wasn't damaged.

"Mr Artindale was politically minded. He was a true blue Conservative. One voting day he told Crofts to bring the car round. He said 'Come on girls, we're going to vote.' Of course Kitty ran to him but I said 'I'm not going to vote.' He was mad. He said 'You flappers should never have had the vote.' I wouldn't vote Conservative. I said 'Sir I don't understand politics and I'm not going to vote.' He was mad but I didn't go. He

**Mr and Mrs Artindale in the gardens of East House, about 1930.**

didn't like me for that. What with that and my involvement in getting Nurse Crowle the sack, I wasn't particularly in favour. He had two reasons to dislike me. He wanted me to go and vote Conservative the same as him. He made sure the rest of the staff voted Conservative. He knew.

"Mrs Artindale used to go fishing too. She'd go to Bournemouth. I've got a newspaper cutting. It reads 'Fishing from Bournemouth pier on Wednesday Mrs Ilma Artindale landed a conger eel of 16lb. On Tuesday the same angler, from a boat at about a mile and a half from the pier, secured a skate of 12lb, another of 6lb, and about 20lb of fish of various kinds. As, a fortnight earlier, Mrs Artindale had, from a boat at about the same spot from which she was fishing on Tuesday, landed a dogfish of 28lb, and a conger of 16lb 8oz, she may be said to have enjoyed better and more successful sport than frequently falls to the luck of deep sea fishers in this neighbourhood. Members of the Bournemouth Sea Anglers' Association got busy after hearing of Mrs Artindale's good catch from the pier on Wednesday, and later in the evening Capt. A. J. Whistler was rewarded with a conger which turned the scale at 10lb.'

"Mr and Mrs Artindale used to catch eels. They used to bring eels home. I had to skin those blighters. They've got a rough skin, a hard skin. I had to stick a skewer through the eel's head, to pin it to a board, and just cut round its neck, then catch hold of the skin and pull it off. I used to deal with all that.

"Mrs Artindale's maiden name before she got married was Handley. Her first name was Ilma. I had to call her 'madam'. Her brother, Arthur Handley, used to be at East House quite a lot. I think she only had the one brother. He had a wife, a son and two daughters. One daughter was called Ruby and the other was called Ilma, the same as Mrs Artindale. Ilma Handley was an actress. When Crowle was off duty, on holiday, Mrs Artindale's brother, Mr Handley, used to come down from London. He stayed. He never wanted to be alone, he always wanted somebody with him.

"Mrs Artindale used to drink a lot. She had a drink problem. Her brother used to drink secretly with her in her bedroom. Mr Artindale kept the keys to the cellar in a drawer in a room but Handley used to pinch them. The night before I left to get married Handley went down to the cellar and got a bottle of champagne and we got tiddly in the kitchen.

"Mrs Artindale used to drink on average a bottle of brandy a day. She got her brandy from Wilson and Kennard's in the Market Place. She used to send Joey Crofts down to get it undercover. She'd tell one of us girls to tell Crofts to go down for the brandy. Artindale knew she drank and they rowed about it. She was also a gambler. Joey Crofts liked a flutter too, and he used to place her bets for her. He was really deceitful to the old man. When Artindale died he left his money tied up because he knew his wife had a drinking problem and he also knew she gambled. She used to back horses a lot. She was frittering the money away. He had her called off once for being in debt for £6,000.

"She used to dress up. She got her clothes from London and Bath. On account of her drinking she was flabby. She had nice clothes but because she had a big fat tummy she never looked smart in them. Unlike him she never went to church.

"She used to be in bed nearly all day some days. She always used to have an onion for her breakfast. Always an onion in the bedroom. She ate a lot of onions. She ate a lot of biscuits too. If they wanted anything in the grocery line they

On a window sill at East House, about 1930, left to right:
Kitty Sawyer, Bob Sawyer and Marjorie Meaden.

Kitty Sawyer, Bob Sawyer and Marjorie Meaden.

shopped at Wilson and Kennard's. Crowle used to do the ordering of the groceries. Crowle used to keep them locked in a cupboard and take the key. We couldn't get at them. If we ran out of anything I had to ask her and she'd unlock the cupboard and get the stuff out. After she left Artindale's employ we used to keep the cupboard open and we could have what we wanted.

"Mrs Artindale never used to have a big meal but Mr Artindale preferred cooked meals. There was a lot of game because everything came off the warren more or less. He used to fish for freshwater fish and if they wanted other fish or seafood she used to go to Bath sometimes for that. Artindale ate his meals in the dining room. He was waited upon. The parlourmaid took the food in. He had a four course meal. He didn't eat a lot really. He rang a bell when courses had to changed. Kit saw to that. Sometimes he'd pass comments about the food. He was very fond of rice puddings but they had to be just right, creamy. He always had jam with his rice puddings. Funnily enough I like jam on my rice puddings today. I suppose I got that from him.

"Mr and Mrs Artindale didn't do a lot of entertaining but sometimes friends would come. A doctor from Bath often came for lunch. When they had company I was always in the dining room as well because the parlourmaid couldn't do it all on her own. It wasn't fair really because I had a lot to do in the kitchen. I had to change from my print dress into my black frock and apron to go into the dining room. We wore a uniform and aprons and caps.

"Us servants had the fat of the land. We ate the same as our employers ate in the house. Artindale fattened a pig. It was killed and the bacon cured. The sides of the bacon were hung up in the kitchen. The hams were in the dairy being pickled.

There was also a Jersey house cow, which Bob Sawyer used to milk. When the cow was in full milk she was milked twice a day and the milk was put in cans for the cream to settle on the top. I used to skim that off every morning. It was so thick you could cut it. It was beautiful. I used to have to make the butter every day. When it was my day off I had to make the butter before I went out. We used that lovely Jersey butter for cooking and everything. The surplus, what we didn't use in the house, used to go over to Jimmy White's, the little shop next to the Rose and Crown at East Street, and Mr White used to sell it.

"The Artindales also had their own chickens. Bob Sawyer used to collect the eggs and they always went into the old man's gun room. He had a rack there. He used to keep count of how many we had. Then they'd come out in the kitchen for me to preserve them in water-glass.

"Mrs Artindale came in the house one day with the cockerel under her arm. She said 'The cockerel is cropbound.' She cut its crop open, let the corn out, and sewed it up again. He was alright. He ran about again. The crop is only like skin.

"I worked all the hours God gave me. We had half a day a week off, Thursday afternoons, and I had to be in by ten o'clock at night. And we had every other Sunday. One Sunday you were out and the other Sunday you were in. But the Sunday we were in we used to go out for a couple of hours in the evening after dinner. I was paid £4 a month. That was top wages for domestic workers. I was paid the first of every month, which meant we lost four weeks' pay each year. That way they only had to pay you for 48 weeks and not 52. We used to pay National Health Insurance, fourpence a week.

"I had to give some of my wages to my mother. She used to come up to East House to get it off me. I used to give her a pound a month out of the four I had earned. Mrs Artindale always gave Kit a cheque for her and me and she used to change it at Kennard's shop or somewhere.

"Mr and Mrs Artindale had several dogs. There was a terrier called Bill. It was the kitchen dog and Mr Artindale didn't like it. He didn't want it in the house. He gave it to me but I had nowhere to keep it. My mother couldn't have it. So, Harold and I took it to my brother's at Henley On Thames. We went there on holiday. My brother kept that dog for years. He got very attached to it. Bill was a lovely dog. I would have loved to have kept it.

"Mrs Artindale would come into the kitchen to see me. She had a little Pekinese dog called 'Come On Steve'. It was named after the jockey Steve Donoghue. Mrs Artindale would wander along the passage into the kitchen and she'd sniff, to smell what I was cooking. Her dog followed behind her and he would sniff too. It was like he had to mimic her.

"One of Mr Artindale's dogs was a black retriever, which he used to take on the warren, collecting the rabbits. He'd go into the garden and let the dog out of its kennel and the dog would walk with him round the garden. At mealtimes the dog sat right behind his chair in the dining room. He could send that dog, this is true, to the egg rack to get an egg. The dog would carry an egg to him and he wouldn't break it. It didn't crack. Retrievers have a very soft mouth. Everyday Mr Artindale would send the dog out to get a biscuit.

"Another dog they had was an Alsatian called Girly. Come On Steve was a valuable Pekinese. They used to feed it whisky to stop it growing, to keep him small. He was a tiny thing and he was dark black. Mrs Artindale used to let Girly and Come On Steve out on the lawn

**In service at East House, Kitty Sawyer and Marjorie Meaden, about 1930.**

to play and one day Girly picked up Come On Steve in its mouth and shook it. She thought it was a rat. It shook the Peke's eyes out. Peke's eyes protrude. They took it to the vet and the vet gave it an anaesthetic. They shouldn't because Peke's have only got small noses and they can't take it. The Peke died. The vet, Mr Webster, at Craven House, by the Obelisk, sent his bill in. She wouldn't pay it because she said he killed the dog. He didn't take her to court. He knew he was in the wrong and the publicity would have cost him his business.

"That was a beautiful lawn at the back of the house and we all had to wear soft shoes to walk on it. Artindales also had a Sealyham dog and the little devil was always scratching holes in the lawn. Mr Artindale came into the kitchen and asked me to mix up a bowl of mustard. I did it, not knowing what he wanted it for. Mr Artindale put the mustard in the hole and rubbed the dog's nose in it. Poor old dog went nearly frantic. Missus was mad. She took the dog up into the bathroom and washed its mouth. Poor dog. He got over it.

"Mr Artindale was very particular about the garden and all that went on around but he wasn't bothered about the house indoors. The walls were painted but they were fairly plain. When the house was decorated, which they had done occasionally, he couldn't stand the smell of fresh paint, so he used to clear off to his club in London and stay there. I forget the name of it. She used to go to Bath to stay an awful lot. They didn't go together. We'd have the decorators in. We used to like that because we'd have about a fortnight on our own. The parlourmaid had a boyfriend and he'd come in for a bit of fun.

"East House was a big place. It had a big hall, as big as a room, with an old staircase that led to the left to the parlourmaid's pantry where she cleaned the silver. It also went to the kitchen. Sir's gun room was more or less opposite the kitchen door. Along the passage were the dairies and the coal house. To the right of the hall was the dining room. From the end of the dining room you could go into the greenhouse where he used to grow roses. That was Prince's greenhouse.

"There was a marvellous grand piano in the hall and long troughs filled with beautiful flowers. Prince saw to them. Mrs Artindale played the piano, sometimes, not very often. The telephone was in the hall, it was an old fashioned one. It was all parquet floors. Bob Sawyer used to polish those with a big square, heavy, polisher. It was a beautiful floor. It was done with beeswax and turpentine. I used to have to do that on the kitchen stove. The floor must have been pulled up when the house was demolished.

"The parquet went right into the billiard room which adjoined the hall on the ground floor. All round the walls in the billiard room they had heads of stuffed animals. It was a lovely room. Mr Artindale had a beautiful billiard table. He used to play billiards a lot. He used to play against Handley, his brother-in-law. Handley played a lot. Mrs Artindale used to play when she was drunk. They used to have a man come down from London with a great big iron to iron the table. When Mr Artindale died his wife gave the table to the Warminster Conservative Club.

"Every Christmas Eve the Town Band played music in the billiard room. I had to cut the sandwiches for them. Mr Artindale always gave them a bottle of whisky, and a pound each. They played for Mr and Mrs Artindale and us staff. No one else. Sir used to give us a bit of money for Christmas but not a lot. He had a tree and decorations in the house at Christmas. Handley's daughters used to come down. Mr Artindale was very fond of Ruby. She was left something in his will.

"The billiard room had big bay windows. There was nothing else in the billiard room. There was a beautiful fireplace in there. It was an open fire with a great big brass fender with a cushion top you could sit on. You could sit on the fender. It was a great big high one built round the fireplace.

"The furniture was very nice in the dining room but there wasn't a lot of it. There was nothing modern about it. In each window were polished troughs filled with flowers. Mr and Mrs Artindale loved their flowers. It was a huge dining room with a big fireplace. Leading off from the lounge was another room, a smaller dining room which they sometimes used.

"They never had a lot of antiques. They had some nice silver but that was never on show, it was in the cupboards in the pantry. They had rugs on the floors. There was carpet in the dining room. They had acetylene lighting. Joey Crofts used to make that up there somewhere. It was on the wall, like acetylene lamps.

"I was quite happy at Mr Artindale's. I liked the job very much, even though it was hard work. I left East House to get married when I was 24. I had been with the Artindales for nearly eight years. I married in 1930. I started for Artindale in 1923. He didn't mind my leaving. When I got married Mr Artindale gave me £5. Missus gave me six weeks rent for the flat we had. It was a guinea a week. She also made me a wedding cake but she was drunk. She put all the liquor going into it. We thought it was heavy. She iced it. I bought another cake as well because I couldn't rely on the one she had made me for the guests. Her's had a horseshoe and a lady with silver bells. I kept that in a glass case for a long time until it got broke and I slung it out.

"Mr Handley gave me a white bedspread as a wedding present. I've still got it at home today. It's never been used. I've tried to sell it. It's a 100 by a 100, embroidered. I've never used it because I couldn't launder it. It's been laundered once. I could wash it but I couldn't iron it, it's too big. Joey Crofts gave me a copper kettle for a wedding present and I've still got it.

"Mr Artindale died in 1933, three years after I left. The newspaper cutting I've got about his funeral reads 'The funeral of the late Mr Robert Henry Artindale took place on Friday morning at St John's Church, and a large number attended to pay their last tribute to the man who had held their respect and esteem during his lifetime. The service was conducted by the Vicar of Warminster (the Rev A. R. Bellars) and he was assisted by the Rev H. Wake. The cortege was met at the churchyard gate by the officiating clergy and the choir, and, as they entered the church the congregation sang the hymn *Let Saints On Earth In Concert Sing*, Mr A. Munday being the organist. The beautiful *23rd Psalm, The Lord Is My Shepherd*, followed, and the lesson was read by the Vicar. Then the hymn, *Peace, Perfect Peace, In This Dark World Of Sin*, was rendered by the congregation, after which prayers were said by Rev H. Wake. The cortege moved out of church to the chanting of *Nunc Dimittis*, and, at the graveside, the committal lines were said by the Vicar.' Then there's a list of mourners and the wreaths. The message on my wreath said 'Heartfelt sympathy, from Marjorie Yeates.'

"Mr Artindale was in his eighties. He made a will with Finch, the solicitor, at Westbury. Rudman and I were witnesses to the will. Not long after Artindale made another will but we weren't called as witnesses. Finch brought his own. Rudman and I were put in that will.

Marjorie Meaden with one of Mr Artindale's dogs.

**Mrs Artindale with Girly the alsatian.**

Handley told us.

"I've got a cutting from a newspaper about Mr Artindale's will. It says '£1,000 for Wilts Church. Bequests of Mr R. H. Artindale, of Warminster. Mr Robert Henry Artindale, East House, Warminster, who died on January 31st last, has left £41,168 6s 11d, with net personalty £35,304 7s 6d. Probate is granted to Arthur Edward Handley, Dover House, Doneraile Street, Fulham, London; Jacob Kelk Marshall, Oak Lodge, Boughton, Faversham, Kent; and Fred James Finch, Westbury. The testator gives East House and furniture to his wife; £250 each to the executors; 26 Doneraile Street, to his brother-in-law, Arthur Edward Handley; £1,000 to the Vicar and churchwardens of St John's, Warminster for church expenses; £250 to Joseph Crofts, chauffeur; £50 each to Henry Rudman (gardener), Kitty Sawyer (housemaid), and Ena Marjorie Meaden (cook) if respectively in his service; and the residue to his wife for life. On her death he gives £1,000 each to his nephew, William Handley, and his niece, Ruby Handley; £5,000 to his brother-in-law, Arthur Edward Handley; £2,000 to Warminster Cottage Hospital, and the residue of the property to Charlotte Rock.'

"I missed out on that will because I had left Mr Artindale's employment before he died. Mrs Artindale later sold the house and went to Bath. Kit Sawyer, the parlourmaid, went with her. Mrs Artindale died at Bath but where's she buried I don't know. After she sold the house it was demolished and the East End Avenue housing estate was built on its site in the gardens [1939].

"I don't think much of Warminster now. I much prefer it where I live in Weymouth. I wouldn't come back to Warminster to live, not on your nelly! I hate Warminster. I don't know why. I know I grew up here and did my courting here but it makes no difference. Harold wanted to come back to Warminster when we retired, but I didn't. I never want to.

"The world is dreadful now, it's a wicked world, it really is. It's a terrible world today. Still, it's not the world, it's the people who live in it. I don't think there's any discipline today. As regards all these murders and vandalism, I think the birch should be brought back. I really do. I'm sure that capital punishment and the birch would change the world for the better. They'd jolly soon stop these muggings and murders. They won't do it, they say it makes people retaliate, they say it makes them worse. I don't believe it. It would do them good. It's got to come back.

"It's everyone for themselves now. It's greed. What is this world going to be like when the younger generation are old. I'm glad I won't be here to see it. People will not go without anything and there's no respect, none whatsoever, for other people's property. Even young kids are doing wicked things. They are not taught to respect things. Victorian values have gone out the window now. We were brought up properly. Television is a lot to blame for what's happening now. Young children sit in front of it and watch it. They think nothing bad of it. That's the world they live in.

"Television would be alright if they put decent programmes on but they put on insulting rubbish. It's not fit to look at. I think it's wrong how these television people and pop stars get all this money. They ain't worth it.

"I don't consider myself wicked and I don't consider myself religious. You don't have to go to church to be good. I like going to church but it's rare I go. I hope to go to heaven. I think if you live a good honest life you're as good as anybody could be. I believe those who are really wrong are repaid eventually.

"Politics? I'd like to choke Mrs Thatcher. I admit she's a wonderful woman but she's not fair with a lot of things. She's a rich woman and she's out for the rich. That's what the Conservatives are all about. I wouldn't vote for them when Mr Artindale wanted me to, and I'm not about to start now. I've never been a Tory, even though I lived with and worked for the snobs. It's wicked what they're doing to the National Health Service. Charity shouldn't have to keep our hospitals open.

"We've got poverty, plenty of it, in this country and we're always sending money abroad to this third world. The third world? We're all one world. If anything goes wrong in this country no one helps us. Yet when there's a disaster or famine abroad we send a million or two over there. You see these Arab princes with their palaces and their gold; they make millions. That's the blighters that should help when money is needed.

"Trouble is the people in these poor countries are not prepared to help themselves. They should be taught how to control the population When we send this help abroad we should put in a leaflet and a condom. Until they stop the increase of the population they are always going to have poverty.

"I didn't know anything but poverty in my younger days. My family was poor. Eggs were only two a penny but we could never afford to have a whole egg each. We used to have half each. Same with an orange, it was half each. We were very poor. My mother and father brought up 14 children. They used to have a child a year. There was no television!

"I had to work hard for a little bit of money. Years ago £5 was a fortune but it's nothing now. What I've got we've had to work for and there's no one but ourselves to thank for it. When we got married we had very little. We didn't have a suite of furniture but Harold used to make things. He was good at woodwork. He made a table and a bookcase. We've still got the bookcase. He used to do odd jobs for people and make a bit of money that way. We never had what we couldn't afford. I've always gone without things. We started with nothing. We've had to work to get what we've got and that ain't much. We've still got two chairs from our first suite of furniture and that was £13. I'm not boasting but no one could say I'm not a good manager. If I wanted something I would save for it. Nobody could make me touch that money. It's like saving for your rates. We wouldn't dream of touching it, we know it's got to stay there to pay the bills.

"People are greedy now, They buy things they can't afford and they get into debt. A young couple that gets married today have got to start with everything. I never had a washing machine. I haven't got one now. I still do my washing the old-fashioned way. I boil it in a boiler. I've got a spinner, mind, and I wouldn't be without that because it does help with the drying. I'm not complaining because I haven't got a washing machine. It's my own fault. I like to go my own way. We didn't have a fridge until our golden wedding. I never wanted one before.

"If I could have my time over again I'd change a lot of things. We never had the opportunities to really enjoy ourselves much when we were young. Still, I've had a wonderful life. Harold and I survive on our old-age pensions. We should get a pension according to the cost of living but we don't. I'm not complaining about it. We manage quite comfortable. We have good food. We don't have a lot of luxuries but we have what we need. We don't smoke or drink, and we spend our money the way we should, not on gambling and bingo. Therefore we can manage on our pension. We live within our means."

# I'D WHISTLE AS I SKIPPED ALONG
## Roy Hampton
*21 April 1988*

"My name is Roy George Hampton. I was born on 27th November 1911, at Bleeck's Buildings, at West Street, Warminster. That's where I grew up. My mother worked in the laundry at the Grammar School, at Church Street, with my aunt and Mrs Trollope. They did all the washing and ironing. My dad worked with his father at Mark Hill's Timber Company on the corner of Imber Road and Market Road [Fairfield Road]. Dad was captain of Warminster Town Football Club at one time, and he was once captain of the Christ Church team.

"When I was five or six I started going to the Minster School at Vicarage Street. Miss Frost was the headmistress and she was very strict. It was absolutely iron discipline. She put us through the mill, mind. Also, there was a Miss Bryant. Her brother Roy Bryant now keeps the shop over at Bapton. Well, later on, there was a teacher at the Minster called Miss Weare and she married Roy Bryant. I enjoyed every minute of it at the Minster School.

"Only a few weeks ago I went down to the Minster School and I walked up the old flagstone path. There was a lady there, I suppose she must have been one of the teachers, and she said 'Can I help you?' I said 'Not really, it's just that I went to school here years and years ago. I'm on a bit of a nostalgia trip.' You don't know the sort of feeling you get when you go back to somewhere that you were years before. This lady said 'Have a look round.' So, I had a look all around the playground. On the edge of Miss Frost's old study the bricks were worn away. That's where us kids used to get up there playing about. The school building hadn't changed much, it was very much the same. We used to have a piece of linoleum all round the classroom and we were allowed to draw whatever we liked on that. The best drawings were kept on there and the rest were rubbed out. They were good old days.

"The Lucas family lived opposite Bleeck's Buildings at West Street. They had a forge. They had a furnace in a big galvanised shed and they'd put the coals on. They did various jobs with iron and steel. Us boys used to have hoops and if one did break we did take it in there and old Mr Lucas would mend it. His son, Austen Lucas, was in the Warminster Fire Brigade. He used to let me clean his brass helmet every week and he'd give me sixpence.

"I can remember one day old Mr Lucas came out of his house and he started putting up flags and bunting. I watched him. I said 'What are you doing that for?' He said 'The War's over.' I said 'The War? What War?' He said 'We've defeated the Germans,' and he shouted 'Hooray.' I shouted 'Hooray' too.

"Austen Lucas was a lamplighter and he'd go round with a little short ladder and a bicycle. He'd go up the ladder and turn the gas on and light it. We used to follow round behind him, climb the pole and put the lamps out. We'd run away and he'd cuss us. He had to re-light them. In the morning he went round and put them out.

"When I was about nine our family broke up. This would be about 1920. My mother and my father separated, and my brother and I were sent away to live in a home. My father had joined the Army. He was in the Argyle and Sutherland

Highlanders. He eventually went to Canada, where he was in the Toronto Scottish Regiment. He's dead and gone now. He died in Toronto and had a full military funeral.

"I was moved to Stockwell and my brother was with me to start with but he left to go to St Leonard's. My brother Bob and I could never hitch it. You get that in families. He was a jump ahead of me all the time, for the simple reason that I had to attend St Bartholomew's Hospital in London. I had ear trouble. That put me back a bit. When I got to St Leonard's my brother had moved on to a farm home and, blow me, I found myself in St Leonard's without him.

"As soon as I got to Stockwell they gave me a haircut and put me in a bath of water. The master came with a towel and rubbed me dry all over. Then he took us into Hastings and had our photograph taken. There were 25 of us boys in Stockwell. And do you know what? Although I say it myself, although the discipline was strict, we got on alright. They formed a Scout troop there and one year we went to Guernsey for a holiday. We had three weeks over there. We did camps, like one at Battle Abbey. You didn't get much to eat, only enough to keep you going. I didn't grow much as a nipper.

"One thing that stands out in my mind, and I can see this so vivid. When I was in the waifs and strays home, the master took us boys up Kennington Road for a walk on Clapham Common. I saw a lorry come up through, open top, full of soldiers all in blue. I asked who they were and I was told 'They're soldiers and they're wounded and they're going to hospital.'

"I spent four years in the home. It was lovely on the South Coast. Eventually, the four years was up and I got sent back to Warminster. One of the Home Committee saw to me, he brought me

**Warminster Fire Brigade during the 1930s when Albert Dewey was Captain.
Austen Lucas is second from the left, middle row.**

**Warminster Town Football Club, 1906-7 Season. Back row: W. W. Sparey, Richardson, C. Waddington, W. Cane, F. S. Foreman, G. R. Langdon. Middle row: J. Curtis, J. Pinnell, Tooley, H. Holton, D. Waddington. Front row: E. Pressley, J. L. Whitmarsh, W. Hampton.**

back on the train and he saw me as far as West Street. He had on a great big overcoat. I had nothing really. All I carried was a great big tin of cigarette cards.

"Funnily enough I had to take the wife down to the Clinic at Westbury the other day to have her feet done. While I was sat there waiting I got talking to another chap. He married a girl Tucker. We had a chat. I said about being in a home as a child. He said 'Where did you go?' I said 'Stockwell and I remember it well. There was a tube station and I saw hundreds of soldiers going through with blue uniforms on.' He said 'I was in that waifs and strays' building in Stockwell.' I said 'You wasn't?' He said 'I was!' You can't believe it, can you?

"When I got back to Warminster I went to Sambourne School. That would be about 1924. Mr Bartlett had been the headmaster but Mr Fred Taylor was the headmaster when I was there. One of the teachers was Albert Saywell. He was a devil mind, he was strict. If you did something wrong he'd bump you all up the aisle between the desks. But I took all that in my stride. I'd love to see him now. Mr Taylor was a very nice man but he was also very strict. He was alright for his job but he could baste you if he wanted to. If you did something wrong you were sent by the teacher to him. He'd have you in and give you a couple of strokes. I have to say this, it was all for your own good. There was also a lady teacher, a big woman, but I can't remember her name. And there was a Miss Davis.

"Before we went into Sambourne School in the morning we played football with a tennis ball. I've got vivid memories of that. We used to play football in the playground. I can 'see' all my old mates now: Bill Brown, Ernie

Lewer, and the others; they're all gone.

"While I was going to Sambourne School I was an errand boy for Webb, the draper. He had a shop in the High Street, on the corner with the Close, across the road from the Athenaeum. I used to take parcels round town for Webb. I didn't find that a chore. I was happy doing that. They used to pay me four or five bob a week. Miss Walters, Miss Bendle, and Sammy Webb worked in the shop.

"Jack Vallis had a fishmonger's shop on the corner of George Street, next to the White Hart. He used to put trestle tables out on the pavement. That was all kippers and bloaters, whatever he had. Sometimes he'd catch hold of me as I passed by with one of Webb's parcels. Mr Vallis would say 'Take these fresh herrings up to Major Mortimer at the Manor House.' That was the big house off Ash Walk. Major Mortimer was the Agent for the Longleat Estate. I didn't mind going up there for Mr Vallis. He'd push a couple of pennies into my hand for my trouble. I was as happy as a sandboy. I used to get on with everybody.

"I loved being about the town, seeing all the sights and watching what was going on. I'd whistle as I skipped along. Eastmans, the butchers, were on the corner of George Street by the old Council Yard. I'd see George Pearce, who worked for Eastmans, sharpening his knife. His mother and father lived up West Street. You could get half a shoulder of lamb for two shillings and sixpence. Further along George Street was Payne's Bakery, next to the Methodist Church. Cecil Turner drove Payne's bread van, and Jim Pressley worked for them too. On the other side of the Church was Foreman and Worthington's. They were upholsterers.

"Miss Francis had a boot shop in George Street. She was short and fat and she was a jolly old soul. She used to wear a black apron. In that shop she had

**The Teichman Hall at Boreham Road, 1987.**

104

leather, and leather soles, nails, little hammers, and all the kit for doing boot and shoe repairs. My mother sent me to Miss Francis whenever our boots got badly scuffed or needed mending. It smelled of leather as soon as you opened the door. You'd go in there. You'd say 'Hello Miss Francis.' She'd say 'What do he want then?' You'd say 'I want some nails for my shoes.' She'd weigh out a little handful on the scales. 'Alright then?' she'd say. She'd wrap them up in a screw of brown paper.

"They were happy days. I used to go to the fun fair. That was held in the main street every April and October. Everyone looked forward to that. It was grand. You saved up a few pennies for it. There were all sorts of roundabouts and stalls. Hardiman from Bristol would have his horses, the gallopers, on top of Town Hall Hill [High Street]. There were coconut shies and darts, and the cake-walk was in Weymouth Street. Jim Summers, the horse slaughterer, would get up in the boxing ring and have a bout with one of the professionals.

"Our road, West Street, didn't have a tarmac surface. It was just dust. The Council used to send round a water cart to dampen down the dust. We used to chase behind and put our fingers over the holes to stop the water coming out. The driver used to lash out with his whip. He'd shout 'Get on with you.' We'd do anything like that for a bit of mischief. We didn't hurt anyone and we didn't do any damage. There was no vandalism. We used to get up to mischief but not vandalism. I didn't see any of that.

"You could go playing all down across Church Fields but you wouldn't go down there on your own today. Something might happen. We used to go playing in the fields behind where Luxfield Road is now. Down the bottom of there was Hog's Well, the river which ran down through from Cley Hill. We used to get down there. Win, my wife, and all her girl friends used to dress up, like kids do, and dance down there. We boys used to pay a halfpenny each to watch them. All of a sudden you'd hear, in the distance, a shout. We all used to dive back up the road. That was Stevanno from Frome with his ice-creams. He had a churn full of ice-cream. We dashed in home and got cups to get ourselves some ice-cream. Stevanno was Italian and he came with his cart to Warminster from Frome every Saturday.

"We used to play 'Dicky, Dicky, Show The Light'. We played that in the fields behind Charlton's shop at West Street. One of us boys would have a torch and he'd set off into the fields, in the dark. The rest of us would shout 'Dicky, Dicky, show the light.' He'd give a couple of flashes on the torch and we'd have to try and figure out where he was. Every couple of minutes we'd have to shout and he'd flash the torch. We'd creep up on him and the first one to find him had the next turn with the torch. That was one of our games.

"Another thing we did was 'Pull Parcel Pull'. We'd put some grass or some stones in a cardboard box and place it by a path. We would tie some string to the box and get back out of sight. Some unsuspecting person would come along, look at the box, and their curiosity would get the better of them. When they went to pick up the box we would tug on the string and pull the parcel away from them. We'd run like hell. One time, a man didn't find it funny and he set his dog after us. Fred Prince and I ran all the way out to Coldharbour on the Bath Road because we were scared. That was our fun.

"We used to do a prank or two. You know where the garage [recently Warren King's but now Eldan Motors] is at Victoria Road? There used to be a house there called Upton House. Mr Jefferies, the glove man, used to live in there. Next to it was a lovely orchard where we used to go scrumping. That was the main thing, scrumping, to get your apples. By the time Mr Jefferies came out to chase us we were gone.

"There were policemen about. They weren't in cars or on bikes. They walked about. If you saw a pair of policeman's black boots coming you got out of the way quick. That way they couldn't touch us. P.C. Sawyer used to live down Pound Street Hollow. Superintendent Barrett was up at the Police Station at Ash Walk, where the Christian Science Church is now.

"When we were kids we were very observant because we had nothing else to do. Bunny Wyatt had a little shop at Silver Street. He came up home one Saturday afternoon. He had a horse and two wheel brake loaded up with apples, oranges, mackerel and haddock. He left his horse next to the railings by Bleeck's Buildings. We were there playing with our tops. I went to give my top a good crack and it went against the horse's hoof. The horse bolted off down the road. Bunny came out, shouting 'Stop, stop my horse.' There were apples all down the road.

"Molly Butt had a shop at the bottom of Pound Street. She was a bit cross-eyed and she wore glasses. She sold liquorice bootlaces and all that. There were coat hangers with old clothes on. Her shop was a real shambles. Molly had a big cat and that damned cat would be sprawled out on everything. On the counter was a great big thing full of black treacle. Mother would give me a basin and say to me 'Go in Molly Butt's and get some treacle.' Off I'd go. Molly would turn the tap on the barrel and the treacle would slurp out. I'd lick it out of the basin on the way home. When I got home mother would say 'Is that all you've got?' I'd say 'Yes, it's gone up in price.'

Mother would give me a bit of bread, no butter on it, to eat with my treacle.

"Mr Bush was the landlord at the Lamb pub at Vicarage Street. He had one arm and he lived in a house on the bash at Pound Street. Miss Burgess had a shop at Pound Street. It was small but very nice. She used to sell sweets. We used to go in there with a halfpenny to spend. And Mr Curtis had a fish and chip shop further up. He used to drive the van for the Castle Steam Laundry at George Street.

"Bob Hill was a bit of a farmer with hay sheds up by what is now Luxfield Road. He had a smallholding. When I was little he used to go out with my dad, with terriers, rabbiting. I used to go into Mrs Hill's shop at West Street to get a few groceries for mother. There would be liver hung up and rabbits hung up. As I got older she always used to give me some sweets or a packet of Star cigarettes.

"My mates and I would go and watch the silent films in the Palace cinema on Saturday nights. It cost twopence. We called it the chicken run. In we'd go with a packet of Woodbines to smoke. A chap from the Station Road area sat there playing the piano accompaniment. Later on we all used to watch Ronald Colman. At the top of Town Hall Hill was a trough and an old gas lamp. The Salvation Army, old Stan Bush from Chapel Street and old Pricey and the others, would all be there singing away at *Land Of Hope And Glory*. We'd stand there and watch them.

"The Reformatory School, up at Tascroft, had one of the best bands going. On Sunday mornings the people of Victoria Road and West Street used to stand outside to watch that band go by. They were young, nice-looking blokes. There were tall ones and little short arse ones marching together but talk about the Guards, they were smart. They marched

**The Wiltshire County Council Egg Laying Trials at Copheap Lane, 1931.**

to the Minster Church for the service. It was a beautiful band. You could hear them coming down the road. After the service they marched all the way back up the road. In the day time the boys had to get out in the fields, hoeing and sowing. It was like a farm school. Those poor boys left that place better than they come there. Mr Jimmy Rutty taught them carpentry.

"During the Depression in the 1920s there were a lot of people out of work in Warminster. The Labour Exchange was next to where the traffic lights are now in the Market Place. Mr Pullin, from Chain Lane or Smallbrook Road, was in charge. I saw the queues of blokes standing about with their hands in their pockets, hoping to get some work or some money. Then you'd see farmer Angell from Parsonage Farm, at Elm Hill, go in, to tell the Exchange he wanted a few men. Then you'd see some of them blokes outside shuffle away. There were some who were work shy.

"Years ago you saw blokes on the road, making their way up to Sambourne, to the Poor Law Institution. Some of them played mouth organs. *I'm Forever Blowing Bubbles* and all that. They used to go in the Workhouse, stay the night, and chop a bit of wood. They used to wear corduroy jackets and corduroy trousers in there. In the morning they were given a bit of bread before they were sent on their way.

"When I was a lad, if I wanted a haircut I would go to Ted Cox's in the High Street. That was an experience. You could sit in the chair for hours. If he wanted a cup of tea he'd go off, halfway through your haircut, and get himself one.

It could be twenty minutes or so before he came back. Then he would have to go and get some tobacco for his pipe, or he'd stop to clean his pipe out. Or he would stand chatting away to somebody. You just sat there and waited. You didn't complain. Time was nothing in they days. Nobody hurried.

"I left Sambourne School when I was 14 and got a job. I started in the nurseries at Harraway's, with a chap named Gerald Curtis. There were others there. This was where the Sambourne Gardens housing estate is now, off Sambourne Road. Harraway's used to have a shop down at Vicarage Street, where Vicarage Street Print are now. There was a chap there called Dick Bull. He used to live up Obelisk Terrace. I had to go in there in the morning and get detailed for what jobs I had to do in the nurseries that day. Mr Harraway would say 'Alright, off you go.' We'd go up Sambourne or up through the Avenue to Copheap, because they had nurseries up there as well. Wiltshire County Council had some land close by at Copheap where egg-laying trials were carried out. I used to see all that going on. I started work for Harraway's at eight o'clock in the morning. You finished at five in the afternoon. You did weeding, hoeing and

**Aerial view with Sambourne in the foreground, 1968. Harraway's Nurseries (now the Sambourne Gardens residential estate) near the centre of the picture.**

**Prestbury House, on the Boreham Road, 1982.**

all that sort of thing. I got about 13 bob a week. No more than that. The wages were very low. You got by. I took my wages home and gave everything to my mother. She'd give me back, maybe, a couple of bob, enough to get yourself a few Woodbines. They were twopence for five. I've always liked to smoke.

"I wasn't earning much money and I wanted to better myself. I wanted to feel happier. I wasn't trained to bud roses or anything like that. I heard of a job going with the Reverend Dixon. He lived at Prestbury House, on the Boreham Road, and he had a big garden. I went up there to try for the job as garden boy. I wanted to work in that big garden. Rev Dixon was a splendid man, a super man, and he knew that I had been in a home and he was good enough to put me on. Rev Dixon was tall and he spoke with a stutter. I saw quite a lot of him. He was a missionary and he used to go to Antigua and places like that. He married a Miss Pigot but they didn't live together. It was

a funny do. Mrs Mills was the cook at Prestbury House. She was formerly Mrs Lawes, a widow. Vi Marlowe was the parlourmaid and she used to wait on tables. She's still alive and lives up Portway. I didn't really get to go in the house, only into the kitchen.

"The gardener at Prestbury House was Paul Curtis and I worked under him. He used to live up Grange Lane at Boreham. He was a crippled man, he had a short stumpy foot. He was a lovely chap and I got on really well with him. There were just the two of us. The garden ran from the road, where there used to be a lot of chestnut trees, round to Smallbrook Farm which Mr Dowding had. It was a splendid garden. There were apple trees and roses and beds of celery.

"We used to mow the lawns on Wednesday mornings. When we did the banks I used to have the mower on a rope. It wasn't a motor mower. Paul used to hang on, and he had this club foot. He'd say 'Go steady, hang on, go steady. You're putting I over.' When we were mowing we'd stop outside the front door and I could see in the nearby windows. You could see the back of the Rev Dixon's head and his pipe smoke going up.

"One day in the winter it was bitter cold and Paul Curtis said to me 'Come on, let's get down to St John's Parish Room, I'm going to light a fire there.' We went down. I always used to do whatever he said. Paul had the key. He took his bread and cheese and I took my bit of bread and jam. We sat down in front of the great big Robin Hood stove and ate our grub. After, we made our way back up to Rev Dixon's and went into the sawing shed to saw up some logs. It was too mucky to get out on the garden. Not long after somebody came up and said 'Mr Curtis, for goodness sake, come quick, the Parish Room has been and blowed up!' The boiler had blown because the steam couldn't get through the pipes. It had blew back. To think that we had only been sitting in front of it twenty minutes before. Well, we shouldn't have been here today. It was a hell of a mess. I shall never forget that. The women from St John's Church used to meet in the Parish Room. It was used for all sorts of dos. There used to be a cup in there, on show. It was won by the St John's Football Club.

"Down behind the Parish Room, at the end of a drive, was St John's Lodge, where Lady Pelly lived. I didn't know Lady Pelly but I knew her gardener. He was a little short man and he used to wear a blue and white striped apron. I can't remember his name but he was a very good gardener. Years ago most people had big gardens. Major Channer lived at Woodcock and he was a retired army officer and he used to have a fruit farm. He used to sell currants, raspberries and everything. He had one arm. The other had been shot off during the War. His gardener was a chap named Doel. I saw this fellow Doel the other day. He must be well over 90 and I love to stop and talk to him. He said 'Hello, how's going on then?' He lived at Portway, Medlicott, I think.

"Boreham Road was quite a well-to-do area. Miss Lyons, one of the teachers at St John's School, lived in Holly Lodge, next to Prestbury House. She lived with her parents. Her father worked on the railway and another Lyons was employed at the Warminster Timber Company. He was known as Tiger Lyons. That was his nickname. Next to Holly Lodge, in Treverbyn, which is now an old folks' home [Abbeyfield], lived Miss Rule. She was a relation to Squire Temple, who was the magistrate. Temple used to wear knickerbockers and he rode a sit-up-and-beg bicycle. I can 'see' him going along the road now. He was one for the ladies.

"Further down Boreham Road was a house called Oaklands and Miss Bradfield lived there. On the other side of Boreham Road, by St John's School, lived Arthur James. He was the sexton at St John's Church. He was very nice. He had a daughter, Mary. Someone else living on the Boreham Road was Mrs Butler who had a hat shop in town. Down the lane between Mrs Butler's and Major Channer's lived Miss Sheppard. Her father had a bicycle shop down by the Old Bell in the Market Place but that was years ago. Miss Sheppard married Edgar Charlton who had a shop up at West Street. His shop was next to where they've made that new entrance, put that road [Grovelands Way] into that new housing estate [Minster View, Norridge View, etc.]. Edgar sold paraffin. He used to go round doing that. He only had one arm but he could turn the tap on and off. What he could do with just one arm was amazing.

"Major Teichman lived in Highbury House. He had the hall, the Teichman

Webb's drapery shop, at High Street, about 1900.

Hall, where the Scouts meet, built. I saw quite a bit of him. He lost his sons in the War. And there was Lady Scobell. She was a big, portly sort of woman. She was smart and she lived in Belmont. She was a wealthy woman and she lived there on her own but she had servants.

"Next to Prestbury House, where the Barley Close housing estate is now, was Dr Beaven's Barley Research Station. I used to see them sowing and reaping the barley. Dr Beaven was involved with the malthouses. I can remember in 1925, just as I was about to leave school, the malthouse at Pound Street caught fire. There was a big fire there. It was a hell of a fire. There were burnt sacks and burnt timbers. The Fire Brigade thought they were it, well, they did their job but it was difficult for them to deal with big blazes.

"Rev Dixon got me a bicycle to ride about but I wasn't allowed to take it home with me at weekends. I was very often sent on errands down town with the bike. I'd pedal off along Boreham Road and down East Street, past all the familiar places. On the corner of Boreham Road and Imber Road lived Mr Foreman and he worked for the Longleat Estate. Opposite the Rose And Crown were Wheeler's Nurseries and Roy Curtis worked in there. That's where Plants Green is now. Wheeler's land used to stretch right over down to the lane that leads to the Park. They used to grow Wheeler's Imperial cabbage, cut them off and put the heads in the drying shed to get the seeds off. They exported seed all over the world.

"Next to the Rose And Crown was Jimmy White's cake shop. It's an antiques

**A field of Wheeler's Imperial cabbages.**

**Crowds at the laying of the foundation stone of Warminster Hospital, 31 October 1928.**

business now [Bishopstrow Antiques]. You went down two little steps into there. I didn't get on too well at home with mother because I had been the apple of my father's eye. No disrespect to mother, because she's dead and gone now, but I couldn't get on with her. I was the odd one out. We used to fall out. I used to say to her 'What about my dinner?' She used to say 'Here's a tanner, go in White's and get yourself some cakes.' That's what I used to do for my dinner. Mr White was a little short bloke. He'd say 'Hello, do you want some cakes, stale ones?' I'd say 'Yes.' That's what I had for my dinner. That's true. I enjoyed them, every crumb. I used to get hungry in the afternoon but I was never one to grumble. Like if someone wanted help I'd give them my last penny. I would.

"The Reverend Horace Wake arrived at St John's Church. He had one eye. He was a first class bloke. A real gentleman. He formed the 1st [St John's] Boreham Scout Troop. Vic Dawkins, Harry House, George Field, Glyn Silcox, Don Pitcher and lots of others, joined. We used to have our Scout meetings in the Parish Room. The Rev Wake came from Norfolk and he used to have his ex-troop of Scouts down to Warminster for a holiday. They used to sleep up in the loft in the barn at Rev Dixon's garden. Rev Dixon said to me one day 'The Scouts are going off for the day, would you like to go with them?' I said 'Yes, I would like to go very much.' He said 'You go.' He gave me some money to take with me. He was just like a father to me. Super. I think he felt a bit sorry for me.

"One day, Rev Dixon came down the garden and told Paul and I that Lord Bath was going to lay the foundation stone for the new Warminster Hospital at Portway. Rev Dixon asked Paul and I if we would like to go and watch. We said 'Yes sir, very much.' We went and watched the ceremony. That was in 1928. A big crowd of people turned out for that.

"Rev Dixon would come down the garden on Friday afternoons, with my money and Paul's. He'd come in the potting shed, put my money down and put Paul's down. We didn't get paid much but if ever Rev Dixon went away on missionary work to Antigua or anywhere he would always bring Paul and me back a present each. That would be a tie or a shirt. He thought the world of me. I looked up to him and I thoroughly enjoyed my time working in his garden. We worked Mondays to Fridays, and had Saturdays and Sundays off.

"I stayed with Rev Dixon for two or three years until I was about 16 or 17, perhaps not quite as old as that. It turned out that I was worth more than he was prepared to pay me. He'd bought me a bicycle and he'd bought me a watch. Paul Curtis said 'Well, young-un, I'm sorry to see you go but Rev Dixon needs someone younger so that he doesn't have to pay so much money.' There was nothing I could do about it. I left.

"I did a bit of work at the Warminster Timber Company. My brother Bob was there. My grandfather and my uncle, Jack Hampton, also worked at the Warminster Timber Company. One day, Major John, who was something to do with it all, a director, decided to hitch a load of carts on the back of the Timber Company's traction engine, *The Pride Of Wiltshire*, and take all the men for an outing. My people went on that and so did Neighbour Haines. That was Mr Haines. Neighbour was his nickname. Years ago everyone had nicknames. All these chaps went up Larkhill way, to Stonehenge, for the day's outing. Father took his bugle with him and kept blowing it.

"My father was working then in the charcoal factory behind the timber works. It had a tall black chimney. They used to hump these great big cages up with timber and they'd come down on rails straight into the burner. They'd burn all that. A couple of mornings after, when the fires had all died down, they used to get all that charcoal out and bag it up. Charcoal was used for several purposes. They used to put so much of that into charcoal biscuits. Charcoal also went for fuel, it burns lovely.

"The majority of the timber for the Timber Company was hauled in by horses and wagons. I can remember one chap, who is dead and gone now, he used to bring the horses and wagons up Town Hall Hill and it was a struggle. He used to beat them horses mercilessly to get that load up the hill. The timber carriages had wide, shiny wheels, no rubber tyres like today. The horses used to sweat and the carters would shout 'Go on you beasts, go on, get up.' Sometimes the language was terrible. They couldn't let them horses rest until they had the load up over the brow. If they stopped half way up they had to go back to the bottom and start again.

"After a stint at the Timber Company, helping the men on the sawbenches, I worked for a while for Maslin's the Devizes builders. I helped them to build those 22 houses at Princecroft Lane, Warminster. Then I went on the Longleat Estate, about 1932. I tried for a job there and I got it. The first job I done was plant, you know Aucombe, there's trees up the top of there but when you come down from the road on the right hand side there is a fir tree plantation; I helped plant them.

"You know where you go out on the Frome Road, you can turn left at Park Gates and go up the road towards Horningsham? On the left are some very large trees. They are 40 or 50 years old. I helped to plant them. I helped clear the ground for them. I liked working with the timber on Longleat Estate, especially during May and June time when the azaleas were out. There was the smell of the resin and turps and cut timber. You'd have a fire going, it was beautiful. When I started I was getting 27 or 28 shillings a week. I was on with Ted Hale, Walt Bassett, Reg Trollope, George 'Betsy' Curtis and Jack Trollope. Ted Hale lived at 66 Jersey Hill, Crockerton. He was in the latter end of the War. He used to wear a slouch hat. He had a bit of a smallholding. He kept a little pony and he had fowls and chicken. He worked hard.

"When I was up at the Canadian Camp at Longleat, Mr Cameron was the forester. He used to ride about in a pony and trap. That was a lovely black horse. He'd ride into Warminster and tie the horse up in the yard of the White Hart at George Street. One day when we were clearing up, we had some Scotch foremen from Glasgow on with us. He said to Jock 'Yer, how old is that young chap over there?' Meaning me. Jock said 'He's coming up 21.' He said 'Well, you let I know when he comes of age because he shall have full wage, 35 shillings a week.'

"Previously, during the First World War, there were Canadian lumberjacks there with a terrific sawmill. My wife Win and her friends, as girls, used to go out there picking blackberries and they took them up there to sell to these Canadians. They took them in the cook-house up there. At Crabtree they, the Canadians, had a lot of mules for hauling timber. Those men used to wear close fitting hats with a maple leaf design on. In Warminster there used to be a bloke called Bill Hughes. When he was a young man he was exempt from the Army and he was on one of the engines pulling felled timber to the sawmills. The engines were on railway lines and you'd hear them coming, chuff, chuff, chuff. The lines ran in from different parts of the estate, across the road and into the sheds.

"When I was working up Longleat I

**Clearing and hauling for the Warminster Timber Company.
The men include W. Bassett and Ned Snelgrove.**

Driver Reg Mole at the wheel of the Warminster Timber Company's lorry, outside Mr Tanswell's garage in the Market Place, 1930.

The gateway into Longleat Park, near Dod Pool, during the 1930s.

got my hand burnt. We were working out by Shearwater, in a field by Bill Buckett's place. There was me, Walt Bassett, and Dennis Curtis. When we were moving timber we had a hollow gun which you filled with powder. You put it in the end of a log and banged it with a hammer. I had an old Carson & Toone hammer I used for that. You then attached a fuse to the powder, lit it and ran out of the way like hell. As I was putting the powder in, a spark from a fire ignited it. Off it went bang, it blew up and took the skin off my hand. It was hot and I was in agony. I spent seven weeks in Warminster Hospital. Matron Clifford was there then. It did smell terrible, it was awful, but the nurses patched it up okay.

"I joined the T. A. The 4th Wilts. I went with them in 1934 to Wareham, with Captain Houghton-Brown. We won a cup there for cross-country. That were something. I didn't mind, I liked being with all the other chaps. You used to get yourself a pair of good boots from Dodges, at George Street, for 15 bob.

"I served in the Home Guard during the Second World War. I was exempt from the Army because I worked on the land. Our platoon, No. 4 Platoon, used to meet at a hut in Johnny Hall's yard off Weymouth Street. Percy Wills was a drummer when I was in the 4th Wilts. Percy and I had to go on duty together, one night a week at Portway. We used to have to guard Portway Railway Bridge. I ask you. One night we saw a terrific amount of planes going over. It frightened us. Another night we could hear the drone of a lot of planes coming, then it seemed like all the sky over Longleat was lit up. They had dropped incendiaries. Some fell on Cley Hill Farm. I think they mistook Cley Hill for Warminster Downs, because there were soldiers camped up behind Copheap. Another night a couple of bombs fell on Corsley, one fell on Carr's Garage and another dropped on the road outside. Harold Macey, Lord Bath's chauffeur, told me what a mess that was.

"The Home Guard was a joke. Mr Hitler had nothing to worry about, he could have come and gone. We had a few rifles and two Lewis guns for the whole platoon. I mean, honestly, we couldn't have done much. Most of us were old men. Captain Waylen was our platoon commander. He used to have the Rose & Crown at East Street, and he was, at one time, the town bandmaster. He was a proper military man. There was Captain John Everett, the local grocer, and he used to go round on a motorbike collecting orders. And there was Bill Marsh.

"I married Ida Winifred Cull. She was a Warminster girl. I had been at the Minster School with her, and we used to send each other love letters in class when we were little. We first lived at Victoria Road, in a little cottage opposite where the entrance to George Whittle's Farm used to be. It's opposite Masefield Road now. One of two cottages there with ivy on the wall. We paid 5 bob a week rent. We got ourselves a bit of furniture from Bob Davis, who had a shop in the High Street. I went to Bristol with Win, my wife, on the train, and got some other bits and pieces.

"We moved out of the cottage and went to another one further up Victoria Road. It faces Warminster and is on the right hand side going to Frome, by the farm. We let that for seven shillings and sixpence a week and then it was sold to me as sitting tenant. It belonged to David George Stephens. He died and it was put up for auction by Mr Harris at the Town Hall on 27th September 1950. I sold it just over 12 month ago for £50,000. I gave just over £41,000 for this bungalow at Prestbury Drive, which left me enough to buy our curtains and carpets, and I also bought myself a little three-wheel car.

"I retired about ten years ago after doing 26 years at the School of Infantry. I applied for a job as a waiter. The fellow, who interviewed me, couldn't fathom me out. He asked me what I had been doing before. I told him I had been working with timber on the Longleat Estate. He looked at my hands. He said 'Are you sure you're cut out to be a waiter?' I said 'Yes, I want to try it and I promise you I'll do my best.' He gave me a chance and I progressed. I took to waiting alright. I even did the flower arrangements for the dinners. I helped at the Beagle Hunt Balls, all the balls. I did it when Princess Margaret came. I got the ISM. I feel good about having that, but so what, I was doing my job. You get paid and you do your job.

"Old age pensioners haven't got nothing to moan about today. They could do with a bit more. It's bills, bills, bills. Yes, we had bills before but things are getting worse. The rates go up and up. The present Government isn't concerned with the likes of me. I think Mrs Thatcher has got too big for her boots. I've always got time for the underdog. If I thought anybody wanted help I would give it with all my heart. Compare the world I knew with the world we live in today. Now you've got bashing, biffing, pinching, and kicking. By Christ, we lived in hard times but we were on the straight and narrow.

"Television is crazy rubbish. And when I see pictures of Iran with the guns going I think why oh why? I believe in God. There's not one night that goes by without my saying a prayer. I believe that someone hears your prayers. Some of these people that go to church every Sunday, well, I think that's routine. Some, not everyone, are very deep but others go just to show off their Sunday suit. I don't go to church but when I go down the churchyard and see my little girl's grave I think that church is mine. I've still got faith in God even though my girl died when she was four. That was God's will. I prayed at the side of her bed. She looked at me and she was just like a little angel. That was up Victoria Road. Win had gone shopping. That was one of the most painful experiences I've ever had was to see my little girl go. She had pneumonia. She said 'Daddy, daddy, lift me up.' I said 'Alright.' She said 'Daddy, lift me again.' I did, and she was gone. I've never experienced anything so heartbreaking. I accepted the situation. It didn't make me anti-God or anti-religion.

"The world has got bad. Wealth and money has corrupted people. It's greed. Those with plenty don't worry about the poor. Who cares about an old lady going along the road with her hands all cold. Personally I'd put a pound in an old lady's hand and say you have it. Money is the root of evil. If you get a lot of it, you can have this and you can have that and then you don't care about anybody else. All they care about then is their selves. It's now I'm alright Jack and bugger you. Money has got the superior side of them. Half of this country is living it up and the rest is all down there, but give me the poor old man or poor old woman any day. You don't need a lot of money for happiness. Definitely not.

"When I look back to my schooldays I realise that our education wasn't sufficient. I wasn't brilliant. I was average. I got through. Be ordinary, be simple, be friendly and nice to other people. I remember Warminster when it was small and you knew everybody. I suppose that's why it was so friendly. Not now. There's so many people you haven't got time to stop and speak with them all. It used to be 'Hello Roy' and 'Hello George', it was 'How bist?' and 'Where's t'other today?' That's how it used to be."

# BLOW YOUR HORN
## May Ede
*23 March 1986*

"I was born in January 1910, at Hastings, but unfortunately my mother died an hour after I was born. She was only 26. My father, at that time, had just got a new job at Weymouth, so he was in the process of moving from Hastings to Weymouth. Being left with a new born baby, what could he do but pick her (me) up and bring her (me) to his mother at Ash Walk in Warminster. So, my grandmother brought me up. Her name was Jane Munday and she was 60 when she took me as a baby just seven days old. I called my grandmother 'mother' until I realised she was my grandmother. I called my grandparents 'mum and dad' for a while and it didn't enter my head that I had a real dad.

"Grandad came from Imber and his name was John Munday. He was a little older than grandma and he worked at Turner & Willoughby's china shop, next to the Town Hall. They sold furniture and china but the shop has since been demolished, making way for a new building. The Halifax Building Society is there now. Grandad worked for Turner & Willoughby's all his life until he retired when he was 70. He got his old age pension. He retired on five shillings a week.

"I don't know where grandad lived in Warminster before he married grandma, after coming from Imber, but he met her at the Methodist Church in George Street. Grandma used to go there. I found that in the archives, in the old church books. They got married and I think they lived at Church Street to start with. They had four sons and the first one was born at Church Street but my father, the second son, was born here in Ash Walk. They had moved here by then. My children were brought up here and that makes the fourth generation to have lived here. I didn't know a lot about grandfather and grandma. I was 15 when grandfather died and grandma passed away a few years after I married, when my daughter Marian was about nine months old.

"I had a happy childhood as people had in those days without the luxuries and the pleasures that we've got now, because we made our own entertainment. All we had was two bedrooms upstairs, this room and the back kitchen. The water, originally, was drawn from a well but that was just a little before my time, because when I arrived they had a tap outside between the three cottages here.

"Mr Oldnell lived in the next door cottage but one. He was a saddler and he worked for Mr Everett in the Market Place. A funny old lady lived next door to me and her name was Mrs Ferris. Then a very precise lady came there to live. I always remember her telling me that she was 'Lord Bath's cousin's widow's friend.' It was about as clear as mud to me. She was very elite but was quite a nice person. Then she died and Miss Gandy came there after David and Dennis Pinnell's father and mother. We've had the three cottages as one ever since.

"The toilet was right up the top of the garden and it was a bucket one. Up to when I was 15 years old, in 1925, that's all it was. Water was connected in that year. That was also the year my grandfather died. My grandparents brought up four sons in this house and how they did it I shall never know.

"My dad was the second of four boys and his name was Arthur Munday. Like I said, he was born in this house (11 Ash Walk) and he had quite a number of jobs but he was always a printer. I presume he left school when he was about 13 and he was an apprentice at the original Coates and Parker's *Journal* office. He went straight to Coates and Parker's when he left school and he progressed from there. He was one who was always out for progressing and improving himself. He then went to Bath and then down to Yeovil. He worked in Yeovil and that was where he met my mother.

"My mother was born and bred and brought up in Yeovil. Her name was Mabel Wall but they always called her May. She had a stepmother because her mother died and left one or two children but I don't know how many. After a few years her father re-married to a widow with children and there was a Mabel among them. So, what they did, because they couldn't have two Mabels in the family, they called my mother May. Even on her death certificate they put May but they had to cross it out and put Mabel because that was her real name. My mother is buried at Hastings and I'm named May after her.

"Father must have gone to Hastings after he married my mother. I know he was 27 when I was born. When I was seven years old father re-married but I had been with grandma seven years and she didn't want to give me up. My father wasn't really all that keen about having me. He would have had me but he was marrying a wife a lot younger than himself and within a year they had a daughter. So, I had a half-sister and her name was Elsie Munday. She married an Irish boy, who she met when she was in the Wrens. After the Second World War was over she made her home in Ireland, in Belfast. They were doing very well and her husband was something to do with Customs and Excise. Unfortunately, she died when she was 40 of cancer. She had one little boy and I lost contact with this only real half-nephew of mine, if there is such a thing, until a few years ago when he came back into my life. He came over to England to my half-sister's friend and she brought him down to see me. So, now we keep in touch, two or three times a year.

"My father never came back to Warminster to live but he came back visiting. I saw him, perhaps, once a year. I went up to see him quite frequently and after my family were born we used to go up and see them. The last time I went up was before the Queen's Coronation and we stopped with them. He eventually lived at Welling at Kent and he finished up working in Her Majesty's Stationery Office in the Kingsway, London. Where he worked in Kent and the area of London I just lost count. He moved about in Kent. I can remember him really more settled as I got more mature and sensible. When I was 14 years old he was living at Northfleet, near Dartford. He was working in Dartford then. He moved from there to Crayford because he was working in London and he could commute much easier. From there he moved up to Walthamstow but my stepmother didn't like it there, so they moved back into the Crayford area again and they were at Bexley Heath. Then, there was a new estate being built at Welling, and they moved there. They moved three times in Welling. He died there. Actually he died in Plumstead Hospital.

"Being brought up by my grandma and grandfather my uncles were more like brothers to me. William was the eldest and he was an apprentice at International Stores, the old one up the town in Warminster, where Payne's is now. He served his apprenticeship there and he left and went to Edmonton in London, where he met his wife who was a Devonshire

**'PHONE 114**            **'PHONE 114**

# CHARLES EDE

## *BUILDER and CONTRACTOR*

Efficient Workmen always employed for all branches of the trade

**SAMBOURNE RD. & WEYMOUTH ST.**

Advertisement for Charles Ede
from the *Warminster Official Guide 1928*.

---

girl. They married and lived in London and then moved back to Devon. They're dead now. Then there was my father, Arthur. The next brother was Albert and he was an apprentice engineer at Carson & Toone's, at their yard off East Street. He left there and he went to some establishment in Calne. I can remember him, more than anything, when he was at Lister's at Dursley. After the First World War he had a milk round for a while. He packed that up when Filton opened up. He was there and he worked on the *Brabazon*. He was an overseer at Filton and he worked there until he retired. Then there was Herbert, the youngest one, who was 21 years older than me and he was still living at home while I was young. He was an apprentice to Foreman's, the tailors and outfitters, and he did tailoring. From there he went to the Midlands, Birmingham I think, I'm not sure, and he finished up at a big outfitters in Middlesbrough.

"All my uncles did well and they all finished up miles from home. One in Devonshire, one in Yorkshire, and one in Gloucestershire. And my father was in Kent. The only time they ever all met was at weddings and funerals. Really speaking, they were like lots of people who lose contact with their relations because of them moving away, but through me living with grandad and grandma I kept them all in touch. I did all the corresponding for them. In days gone by people were not quite so educated as we were at our age. So, I was the one who kept all the family in contact. I've always kept in contact with all my cousins.

"I started school at the Close,

May Ede's home - 11 Ash Walk.

Warminster, in Miss Trollope's department which was the babies' school. That was in the part of the building that's falling down now. There's a bit on the right of the Chapel and that was Miss Trollope's domain. I can only remember Miss Trollope. There was another teacher but I can't remember her name. Miss Trollope, all through my life, has stood out in my mind. She taught me and she taught my children. I always remember my daughter saying to her one day, when she must have been getting on, 'Miss Trollope, you don't look a day older than you did when I started school.' I said 'Between you and me, she doesn't look any older than when I started school.'

"I was about five when I started school and I was at the Close until they moved us round to the Girls' British School at North Row. We were mixed at the Close. The boys were moved into the other section, the other side of the Chapel at the Close, and the girls went round to what is now Dewey House in North Row. That was the Girls' British School. I should think there were about 80 of us there, because Warminster wasn't so large then. Of course there was the other school, Sambourne, which took girls but I don't know if there was another senior school or not.

"I moved round to Dewey House when I was seven or eight. I can remember being there. It was quite nice and the teachers were teachers then. They were a different type and you respected them and what they said. You thought more of them than you did your home people, really, because their word was law. I was never in the presence of the headmistress because she died before I got there. She was a Miss Ashton and if I remember rightly she came from Trowbridge. She was a wonderful headmistress. There was one teacher that I was very fond of and that was Miss Bindon. She got married while I was still at school and she became Mrs Harvey

122

Taylor. She died not too long ago at Sambourne and her husband was a school teacher. Miss Bindon was a lovely person. She taught me and she taught us all subjects. You had one teacher and she taught us everything.

"My first teacher at North Row was Miss Hayward. She took the first class. She was shorter than Miss Bindon and she came from Trowbridge as well. She was very nice but she was, maybe, a little bit more strict and sharper than Miss Bindon. She was quite a pleasant looking person. She married a Mr Keeping and they had a son called Roy. I think Dick Turpin, who retired from the Reme not long ago, is, or his wife was, some distant relation to them. Miss Hayward was nice and she was a good teacher. Again, she taught all subjects. I had Miss Hayward first and then Miss Bindon. In between, I can just remember, for a short while we had two, what they called, pupil teachers. One was Miss Bessie Hunt and the other was Miss Phyllis James. They taught us before they went to college, but the three proper teachers were Miss Hayward, Miss Bindon, and the headmistress Miss Ashton.

"I found school exciting. Dewey House was one big square room with a curtain across the middle. There were two huge tortoise stoves, one at each end. The north end is where Miss Hayward used to teach us. On the other side was a big sort of raised platform that went up in tiers. We always used to have singing lessons on there. We would be singing there while children next to us would be having lessons. The other side of the curtain was Miss Bindon's class and on the other side was Miss Ashton's class. In between there was a door leading out into some very primitive cloakrooms and some even more primitive toilets at the back which always got frozen up in winter. We had a little play yard, which is still there now. They were really happy days and I enjoyed myself.

"I remember the singing more than anything because we didn't have a piano. We used to have to do the tonic sol-fa, and the teacher would put up her hand in different ways for do and ray and me and all that. We used to sing little songs like *Charlie Is My Darling* and we sang scales. I can remember singing some of the songs. I can still remember one Miss Trollope taught me. It went 'Sleep, baby, sleep, your father tends his sheep, your father shakes his something tree, a little dream drops down to thee, sleep, baby, sleep.' I remember that, ever so plain.

"I can remember when I was a schoolgirl. I don't know if it was Empire Day or what we were celebrating but all the schools marched all through the town. We all assembled in the Market Place around the Morgan Memorial Fountain, which is in the Park now, and each school was dressed up. I was wearing a white dress. My friend, Mabel Dodge, used to go to Newtown School at the Common and they all had paper parasols like you have in Japan. They were carrying them and twirling them. What it was in aid of I don't know but we walked all around the town. Whether we had a band or not I can't remember, and we might have had flags, but I haven't the foggiest idea what we were doing.

"I can remember when the Armistice was signed at the end of the 1914-18 War. We had all gone to the Congregational Church in the Close for a thanksgiving service. We were coming home, my grandad, my grandmother, myself and someone else, and we saw the soldiers breaking all the pub windows at the White Hart in George Street. They just went mad. Either they weren't going to the War or they had been and weren't going back. They broke the windows there in jubilation. The soldiers broke every blessed window in that place. They just went berserk. There were some

Mr Randall talking to Sergeant Marks, at George Street, during the early 1920s.
The photograph was taken by Claude Willcox.

Emwell Street, prior to the demolition of the cottages
between the Weymouth Arms and the Minster School.

people at the pub with the name of Wickham. They had two daughters, Alice and Phyllis, and Phyllis was deaf and dumb.

"After Miss Ashton died we had one or two temporary teachers at North Row but I can't remember their names. I wasn't taught by Miss Ashton. Miss Bindon married before I left there but I can't remember who took her place because when I was 13 we were all muddled up again. There was a big upheaval and all the girls and boys were mixed up again. The babies' school that we went to into the Close was brought around to the Girls' School in North Row and the girls were taken back to the Close again and mixed up with the boys. I was only back at the Close for one term. We went back after the summer recess and I left at Christmas. I was 13 when I left and my 14th birthday came in the Christmas holiday. School leaving age was 14 then, but I left a week short of my 14th birthday.

"I was at home for about nearly a year helping grandma. She was getting on and was seventy-something. Then I went to work at Hibberd's for three and a half years. Hibberd's was a drapery, haberdashery and millinery shop in the Market Place. The shop was where Bateman's, the opticians, is now, next to the Midland Bank. When I was at Hibberd's or maybe just before, the Midland Bank site was Stiles' Bros., the ironmongers. Hibberd's was a very cold shop. It had gas lighting but it never had any heating during the winter. I did an apprenticeship. The first year you did haberdashery, which was needles, cottons, ribbons, and all those sort of things. You looked after those and the next year you did what was called general things and Manchester stuff. Manchester stuff was blankets, curtains, sheets and anything cotton that came from Manchester. We had a room called the Manchester Room and I think that eventually became the Warminster Registry Office. Then, in the third year of the apprenticeship, you branched out into millinery and that was hats, dresses and coats. I did the three-year course and after they kept me on for six months as an improver. Then they couldn't afford to keep me, so I was sacked. I started off at Hibberd's at half-a-crown a week, then it was five shillings, and then it went up to seven shillings and six pence. Improvers got 12 shillings and six pence, and they couldn't keep you on after that.

"The boss at Hibberd's was Mr Christian. He wasn't too bad to work for. I knew him through being at the Methodist Church but that didn't make any difference in the shop. He lived at Pound Street, in a nice red brick villa, I think it's called Talbot Villa, on the corner leading into Princecroft Lane. He had a daughter called Gwendoline. There were some nice girls at Hibberd's. With me at the time when I worked there was Miss Mabel Searchfield, who died not long ago, and she lived at Chapel Street with some of her relations. There was also Joyce Pearce and she was living up Sambourne Road when my parents were alive. Then she finished up living over the shop because she took it on as manageress when Mr Christian packed up. Evelyn Pollard was there with me. She's Frank Whitmarsh's first wife's sister and she's still alive. I was the only apprentice there because they only kept on one at a time. When I was about to leave Winnie Dawkins came on as an apprentice. She's Mrs Robert Scott now. She came on under me for about six months or so. She was there after I left and when her apprenticeship was up she went on for Style and Gerrish's at Salisbury.

"After leaving Hibberd's I was out of work for about two months and then I went to work at Payne's which was a complete contrast. I couldn't carry on with the same trade because there were no other drapers and milliners in the town to work for. I went to Payne's when I was 17 and a half years old. They were a grocer's and pork butcher's at George Street, next to the Methodist Church. I was there for four and a half years until I got married. Payne's was a different kind of life altogether. I was in charge of the cakes and the sweets section but I served on the grocery side too. It was a mixed grocer's shop and we sold everything. It was a good old-fashioned shop and we sold bread, cakes, sweets and groceries. The other side was a pork butcher's and they killed their own pigs and did their own chitterling and all that.

"There was a bakehouse at the bottom of the yard and they baked their own bread. I used to have to put the order into the bakehouse each day for what I needed in the cake line, for special cakes and things. We used to have to weigh every loaf that we brought up from the bakehouse to put in the shop. They had to be the correct weight in case the weights' inspector came round. There was a two pound loaf and a one pound loaf. The two pound loaf cost four pence and the one pound loaf was twopence-halfpenny. Buns and cakes were seven for sixpence. The night before Good Friday we'd be working up very late getting hot cross buns all ready and packed up for the roundsmen to take out.

"Old Mr William Payne was dead before I went there but his widow used to come down in the mornings to help. The owner then was Mr Ewart Payne and his wife. She helped in the office. Mr Ewart Payne was the boss and he was easy going. He was quite a pleasant sort of chap and he was a bit on the plump side. The Paynes were members of the Warminster Operatic Society and she was a wonderful pianist. They had a grand piano upstairs, above the grocery shop, where they lived, and in the mornings she got up there and played for about an hour. It was beautiful and she was a marvellous pianist. The shop and the house was a rambling old place.

"With me, was a Mr Dossett, and he lived at Myrtle Avenue, off West Parade. He had two sons and a daughter. His wife died while I was still there and he married again. He looked after the grocery side and did all the ordering of what we wanted. In the pork butchery side was Mr James. He got the 'flu' and an awful cough. He caught a germ and went deaf. He came from away and I think he lodged with somebody named Harris in West Parade but I'm not sure about that. Old Mrs Payne helped him in the mornings. In the bakehouse there was Mr Cousins, who was the head baker, and there was Mr Sharp and Mr Sharp's son Jack. That was the three in the bakehouse.

"Payne's did a lot of breadrounds in Warminster and they went all round the villages as well. On the breadrounds were Mr Cecil Turner, Jim Pressley, Frank Carter and Gunner Bridle. I don't know why we called him Gunner. They had horses and carts for delivering the bread. Jim and Cecil did the town rounds and it was most convenient to have a horse and cart for that. They would load the cart up and go all up through the town delivering. They could leave the horse and they'd deliver each side of the road, and the horse would move along with them of his own accord. As he saw them move on, so he would move on. When they got to the top of East Street, Cecil would go down the Furlong. They'd meet the horse and cart at the other end, the Fairfield Road end. Mind you, we didn't have the traffic then like it is now. Frank Carter was the first one who went mechanised. Payne's had a big car and they had it converted. They turned that into a delivery van and Frank

Carter drove it. It was an Armstrong-Siddley and they used that to deliver round the villages. They used to go out all round Shearwater, Long Ivor, Longbridge Deverill and Crockerton. They also went out in the Wylye Valley, to Codford and places like that. I don't think they went out to Imber but they used to go right out to the Mud Cottages on the downs, twice a week. Gunner went up and he had a horse and an open cart with a bit of a lid across the top and he carried the bread in that. I remember once he got up there and the horse ran away and he was stranded up there.

"The fire-engine used to be pulled by horses. There was a fire once when the fun fair was on in the Market Place. The firemen had to go up to Smallbrook to catch the horses to put them in front of the fire-engine. I must have been very small but I can remember when what I call our first proper looking fire-engine arrived. Mr Albert Dewey was the captain. I went to school with his daughter, so I remember him. I was Britannia once in a play and I borrowed Mr Dewey's helmet to wear. I padded the top up with newspapers to keep it on. Once there was a big fire in Emwell Street and Harris' Mineral Water Factory got burnt down. I could see the factory burning down from here in Ash Walk. I haven't been round Emwell Street for years. The last time I went round there I think Cruse's galvanised shed was still there. I think there's some houses built there now.

"There have been quite a few changes in Warminster. Take the Market Place for instance. I can 'see' things now. The KTS, that was King, Tanswell and Siminson. They had an organ shop on the corner of Market Place and Station Road. In the middle of their premises was a garage. Eversfield House, where the Gateway supermarket is now, is where Mrs Joyce did dressmaking. She was like

**The commencement of building at West Parade. Back row, left to right: Charles Ede, Clifford, A. Grist, B. Baverstock, F. Chapman, H. Curtis, B. Hughes, C. Waters, F. Moody, T. Ferris, B. Withey. Front row, left to right: C. Pinnell, A. Elloway, H. Franklin, F. Adlam, F. Rowe, W. Elloway and L. Elloway.**

a court dressmaker and she did things for high-up people. I remember going in there to see Lady Mary Thynne's bridesmaid's dress which she wore when Princess Mary got married. She was Princess May really but they called her Mary. Lady Mary Thynne was one of her bridesmaids and her dress was on show in Mrs Joyce's drawing room. Mr Joyce had a photography business. Mr and Mrs Joyce, before living at Eversfield House, used to live at Silver Street. Payne's shop used to be International Stores. The Anchor Hotel has always been more or less the same. Where the Wessex Discount Store is now, that used to be Mr Everett's leather shop I think. He used to do leather work and he used to make horses' saddles.

"I can vividly recall when the teams of eight horses pulling wood, big long timber, belonging to Mark Hill's Timber Company, used to get along in the pitch darkness. The Timber Company was up where the Water Board have a depot now, up by Imber Railway Bridge. It must have been awful in those days for the men doing that job. Starting early in the morning they would walk right out to, perhaps, Longleat or Southleigh Woods or somewhere, and walk those horses back in, hauling the timber. I used to see them coming into Warminster when I was 11 or 12. Sometimes they would go through the Market Place when the fun fair was on. Of course the horses were shy of the roundabouts, so the music would be turned off to let the horses pass by.

"The fun fair came to Warminster twice a year, in April and October. It was held all through the main street, from the Post Office to the Athenaeum, and it used to go down Weymouth Street a little way because they always had the cake-walk down there. I remember that. It was very much like the one they've got at Blackpool now. It was like a moving floor, going backwards and forwards, and you got jogged along. I used to like going on that but I didn't like switchbacks because I couldn't bear things that went

**Members of the George Street Methodist Church on an outing during the 1930s.**

**The Christian Science Church at Ash Walk, 1986.**

up and down. It used to smell like a fair years ago because they used to have oil lamps. There was a thing that came down with a jet on the end and up top was a tin can with the paraffin or fuel in. That was lead down through a tube and came up to a naked flame. That used to smell nice.

"I can remember when I was a tiny girl my grandfather used to go to see the pictures at the fair. Of course we never had a picture house or anything in Warminster then and this would have been the first time we had moving pictures in the town. I can remember it as plain as yesterday. They used to show the pictures in a stall which was always on top of Town Hall Hill. The fair came as far as there because going down the High Street the road got narrower and things got out of balance. They used to site the stall for pictures just past the trough there. There's a bit of a slope there which allowed them to arrange the rows of seating, each row slightly higher than the other. It was also pretty wide just there. I never went in to see the pictures. I was too young but grandfather loved to go and see them. Outside were dancing girls, dressed all in pink, encouraging people to go in. They were like Moulin Rouge girls.

"At each fair there would be a boxing ring but I can't recall much about that.

My hubby told me they used to challenge the spectators to go in and fight the man in the ring. Jim Summers, from up Portway, used to have a go. As well as the boxing ring there were coconut shies and attractions like the fat woman.

"There were sweet stalls and you used to get lovely humbugs. You got all sorts of sweets but I can always remember them making those old-fashioned mint humbugs, bullseye things. They'd make this gooey stuff and throw it up on a hook and pull it. It was like a big butcher's hook. Then they'd put some black in it to make the stripes. They'd pull it and keep throwing it up and down on the hook. I was always fascinated by the way they made those humbugs and they were big humbugs too. They'd throw the mixture up on the hook and they never missed. It wouldn't be considered hygienic these days but we didn't die, we're still alive.

"Benny Withey, in Warminster, used to make sweets. He was a good one for that. At one time he worked for my father-in-law, in the building trade, but I knew him before that because I used to go down to Warminster Common to play with a friend who lived two doors away from him. That was when I was a girl. Benny Withey was quite a character.

"When I was a teenager, between 15 years old up until I was married, we made our own entertainment by having lovely concerts and things at the Methodist Chapel. We had a girls' class run by Mrs Willoughby and we used to meet once a week in the evenings because most of us were working during the day. We used to have what we called the Wesley Guild. It's packed up now like a lot of the things to do with Methodism have but it was really very interesting. Meetings were held every Thursday and there were four different subjects. One would be a divinity evening, when there would be a religious discussion. Then you'd have a literary evening, when you would all discuss a book. Another time you'd have an art evening, and always, once a month, we had a social evening when we used to play some good old-fashioned games. We used to play a game called 'Winking'. You would all sit round in a square with all the girls in the middle and all the boys around the back. There was always one girl's chair left vacant. One of the boys, anybody, could wink at the girl who was sitting in front of him. She then had to run over to the empty seat and the fellow behind her had to try to stop her but he always had to stand with his hands behind his back. But if you, the girl, winked, he had to go and grab you quick to stop you going. If you were quick you ran over to the chair. Then it was his turn to wink. It sounds really funny but we used to have some good times. We had outings too. Of course charabancs had come in by then. Sometimes we had a tour around the Savernake Forest or we'd go to Weymouth or anywhere like that.

"You know there's a place with like chapel doors at Weymouth Street. It's the old Building Essentials place. Mrs Willoughby's house was the house next to there [Weymouth House]. We used to go there on Monday evenings and we called it evening class. We had discussions and we used to practice for concerts. That's where we practiced *Maid Marian and Robin Hood*, which we later performed in the garden of 6 George Street. I loaned you a picture of that for your *Old Postcard Album Of Warminster* book.

"Next to Mr and Mrs Willoughby's was a bit of a garden. It's a pub car park now. Next to there was a house and that's where there was a glove factory. I can remember going through there as a small girl and seeing all the girls working on the machines making gloves. Next to there was the Bunch Of Grapes. It wasn't exactly a pub. It was more select and it sold wines and spirits. It was a bit up-market. The King's Arms was next to

**Benny Withey.**

**The George Street Methodist Church, 1911.**

that. Eventually the King's Arms took over the Bunch Of Grapes, and it's all one pub now, the King Arthur. After the Glove Factory moved out of the house and went up Station Road, the bottom bit of the building was let as flats. I got a feeling Mr Willoughby bought it and turned it into flats. When my husband's eldest brother and his wife got married, they had a flat there but they weren't there very long.

"We had a concert party and we used to go to the different churches in the area. We had some hilarious times. We used to do sketches and we had one or two singers who did solos and duets. We used to take our concerts to the Westbury Methodist Church, to Bradford On Avon, to Wesley Road at Trowbridge, to Wylye, and to Frome. Off we'd go. Sometimes we went in Button's old furniture van and sometimes we went by charabanc. People were beginning to get cars then and occasionally we went in them. Usually we went by Button's charabanc. Mr Button was a big Methodist. Once we went to Trowbridge to do a sketch and we had all our costumes in a big tin trunk. Now, whether it was on top of the vehicle or on the back I don't know but when we got to Trowbridge we discovered that the trunk was missing. It had fell off, so Mr Button had to go back and look for it. Evidently it had fell off near the Rising Sun pub at North Bradley. Somebody had taken it into the pub. We got it back. We used to have some really good times. To people these days it would seem very tame but we made our own entertainment and we thoroughly enjoyed life. It was all good fun and I think, really speaking, they were happier days than what children have today. Now, because they get so much, they don't know how to or bother to make their own fun. When I look back I feel we had a happy life.

"I also had some nice times at work, at Payne's, and I got married from there when I was 22, on 4th June 1932. I got married and I continued to live here at Ash Walk with grandma. By then she was eighty-something and I always felt that she gave up her life to look after me and I couldn't go away and leave her then.

"The year I got married, 1932, the Police Station moved out of Ash Walk. When I came back off my honeymoon the Police had moved to Station Road. There used to be three policemen. They were the superintendent, the sergeant and the one we used to call the ostler. They used to have horses and the ostler looked after them. When I was a little girl there was a Superintendent Scott. Then there was Superintendent Brooks and he used to drill the policemen like soldiers in the field where Manor Gardens is now. I think he thought he was in the army. He used to get the policemen marching up and down Ash Walk like soldiers. That was when I was eight or nine. I can remember that. There were quite a few policemen because the village ones used to come in. I suppose there were a dozen and a half. Brooks was the only one I saw doing this drill, I never saw one do it before and I haven't seen one do it since.

"The Police Station at Ash Walk later became the Christian Science Church, which it still is now. It was three houses. Where the main doors go into the church now, was the entrance to the police station which was only one room on the left. I don't know where the cells were. On the right was a sitting room and the kitchen was at the back. The ostler had two rooms and a kitchen cum dining room. The front door was on the side and it's still there now. The middle house was where the sergeant lived and the door is now blocked up and there's a window in it. They were only two up and two down places. They kept the horses in a place up behind in a nice building. That was turned into a garage later when they got cars for the policemen. They used to keep the straw for the horses up above. When the building was sold and the Christian Science Church bought it, they knocked it about and changed it.

"I can remember a few sergeants. There was a sergeant Northeast. Then there was somebody with the name of Mr Thomas and he lived in the ostler's house. I didn't mind the police. I finished up in the arms of more than one policeman. It was so funny. When I was going to school or working at Payne's I would always leave home at the last minute and I'd go running down Ash Walk. Corrymore, a big house, was on the corner of Ash Walk then and there was only a small gap of a couple of feet because a great big telegraph pole stuck up there in those days. Policemen used to wear big silent boots. One would be coming along George Street and I would be coming down Ash Walk, running like mad, and we'd bump into each other on the corner. I finished up more than once like that. I remember saying to one once 'Why don't you blow your horn when you're coming?' I got used to them and I didn't take any notice of them. There was one, a lovely superintendent, the last one that was there and that was Superintendent Barrett. He was a real saint. He was a Methodist. He was always very nice and if he could do a kindness or help anyone he would. He was really nice and he was the last one at the old police station. A week before I got married he bought me a present and when I got back off my honeymoon the police had moved up Station Road. I remember going up there to thank him for the present. I took him up a piece of wedding cake. He was living in the first house up Station Road then. When he retired he lived at Church Street. His widow died a few years ago.

"My hubby, who I had met, was working in Warminster because his father had a business here. My husband was

Rowland Ede, the second son of Charles Ede who came down here when the West Parade council houses were built. Charles was a Stoke-On-Trent man and he came down here as a builder. He had a builder's yard at the back of the Town Hall, in what was called the Shambles, where those little shops in Weymouth Street are now. He had an extra little bit of yard down where Regal Court is now in Weymouth Street. The Regal Cinema was built on there. He had a little builder's business and he built quite a number of council houses in West Parade.

"My husband was about 13 when he came to Warminster and his family lived in the first council house on the right going up Sambourne. When my husband was about 17 or 18 his mother died and the family had a housekeeper. Mr Ede still kept his business going but he re-married and moved on down to Milford-On-Sea and started a business down there. The eldest son, Sidney, kept the business on in Warminster and my husband worked for him.

"Charles Ede had four children and they were Sidney, Rowland, Andrew and Godfrey. Andrew and Godfrey went to the same school as I did, at the Close. My husband might have gone there but I can't remember. Sidney was old enough to run the business here and hubby worked for him. By the time Andrew was old enough to come into the business his mother had died and Mr Ede's sister took him back to Stoke-On-Trent. He was apprentice to an electrician in Stoke but came back here after a while. He went on to Milford-On-Sea where grandad Ede and his second wife had gone. Andrew got himself a job down at Milford. Godfrey, the youngest son, was apprenticed to engineering and he worked at Wellworthy's at Lymington. So, really, only two of them, Sidney and Rowland, joined the business but it had to close during the Second World War. Everyone was being called up and there wasn't much building going on. That was the end of that. The elder brother went down to Lymington and got in at Wellworthy's on armaments, and the other one was down at Milford. The business never got going again because they all changed their jobs, changed their lives, accommodation and everything. It wasn't the same after that.

"My husband stuck to building work all his life. He wasn't called up during the War on military service. He had passed A1 for the RAF but they never took him because he was more useful repairing bomb-damaged buildings. He was on for Holdoway's and they amalgamated with Parsons for the War. When Bath was bombed so badly my husband was down there for a time because he was in the Red Cross helping with casualties. During the daytime he was sent to work on bomb damage. After a while, London was getting hit so badly, he was sent up there and he was in London for about three years, in charge of about 400 men working on bomb damage. He was in charge at Wimbledon. He came back after things had settled down, a year or so after the War, and he stayed on with Holdoway's in this area. Eventually he left Holdoway's and he went on for County Hall.

"Life during the Second World War was quite exciting. We knew war was coming because the year before was touch and go. There had been the Munich Agreement when Neville Chamberlain came back with the agreement from Hitler that he wouldn't start a war. There was a picture of him in the newspaper coming down off the aeroplane, waving this piece of paper saying 'No war in our time.' Within a year we were at war but we knew it was coming. I can remember the outbreak of the War as plain as if it were yesterday [3rd September 1939]. We didn't go to church because we stayed home to listen to the wireless. We were anticipating something was going to happen. We normally would have gone to church but an ultimatum had been made for 11 o'clock that Sunday morning. Neville Chamberlain was Prime Minister. If we didn't get an agreement by 11 o'clock on that particular Sunday we would be at war. We waited and we heard Neville Chamberlain say 'We are now at war.' They had waited and no agreement had been forthcoming. After the announcement on the wireless my husband and I and our daughter Marian in her pushchair, walked up town and we met some friends. We discussed it, one thing and another, and though we expected it, it was like death. When it comes it is still a shock.

"I could never understand why the radio was called a wireless because it was nothing else but a box full of wires. I've got a feeling our wireless was a tiny thing my husband made in his shed. It was homemade and it was a very old-fashioned sort of a thing. We didn't have electric radio. You had to get the accumulators re-charged. We got that done at Monk's, who had a little shop next to where the Fish & Fruit Company are now in the High Street. It's a little shoe repair place now. Wally Monk had a shop there and we used to take our little batteries down there to have them re-charged. We did this every now and again, depending on how often we had the wireless on. We didn't listen to it a terrible lot. During the war years there wasn't a lot on, only Tommy Handley and folk like that, and there used to be news. We didn't listen much because we were always busy. We were living here with grandma and she didn't like the wireless.

**The interior of the George Street Methodist Church, 1911.**

She couldn't understand it and she thought it was something evil. She wouldn't let us listen to anything that was hilarious because it wasn't in keeping but she did enjoy church services on it. I'm afraid we were rather naughty. We used to tell her that there was a service coming on and it would be Tommy Handley and we'd put it on and she wouldn't know the difference. Her mind was going a little bit near the end. I used to enjoy listening to Tommy Handley.

"For the first year the War was really a phoney thing. We had to get blacked out and all that but I don't think we were rationed straight away. That gradually grew on us. To begin with nothing really exciting happened around Warminster apart from the soldiers getting called up. It was not until the second year of the War that we noticed things starting to move. At the start you never knew it here, apart from the news and the soldiers going through. Towards the end it warmed up a bit. I think what brought things to a head was when Hitler bombed Coventry.

"Actually, at the time, I had soldiers' wives stopping here. We used to get a lot of soldiers sent to Warminster for training. They were here for so long, stopping at what is now the School of Infantry, although it was nowhere so large as it is now. The wives would come down to visit. We had Marian in our bedroom and I often let a soldier's wife stop here in the other bedroom. We had quite a few stop here during the War. We'd have one come and her soldier would tell his pal 'When my wife goes back I know somewhere your wife can come' and we'd get another to stay. I felt I couldn't say no because I might have been in the same position myself one day. My husband might have been landed somewhere and I might like to go and see him. I was really fortunate. The wives stayed about a week. Most of them were working and I couldn't have anyone with a family because we only had one bedroom to spare. I didn't charge them very much. I charged them about £1 10s. They could get their rations and I cooked for them. I kept in touch with quite a few of them for some time.

"We didn't do too badly with rationing. We never had any luxuries but we made our rations go round. The children used to get their sweets and I have always dealt with Miss Waylen, ever since I was married. She had a little sweet shop on the corner of Sambourne. It's now part of the White Hart Pub and I think Joy Bishop, the hairdresser, moved in there after Vera Waylen moved up to where she is now in the High Street. The Rural District Council offices were there in the High Street before they moved to Craven House at Silver Street. I was a regular customer at Miss Waylen's and she always saved me the two ounces of sweets you were allowed for each child. So, the children always had a few sweets. Sometimes I might get the occasional banana. Everybody was in the same boat but I think we lived alright. I didn't know anybody who could get me anything on the cheap.

"I always remember once during the War I went to Bath one day with my daughter when she was about three. We got on the train at Bath to come back. There were a lot of civilian fellows in the carriage. You had to pull the black-out down and we were all sitting together in the carriage. Though you were travelling with all these people you didn't feel frightened of them like you would on a train these days. Opposite me was a nice chap and he spoke to me. He said 'How far are you going madam?' I said 'I'm going to Warminster.' He said 'That's where I'm going. I'm going to Sandhill Camp at Longbridge Deverill.' I said 'I know Longbridge Deverill. I've heard of Sandhill Camp and I know of Sandhill

May Ede relaxing on holiday.

Farm but I can't say I know the camp itself. I know Longbridge Deverill very well because I live in Warminster.' He said 'Is it very far, Sandhill from Warminster?' I said 'A couple or three miles at the most.' I always remember him saying to me 'Are there many theatres in Longbridge Deverill?' I said 'You're going to get a very rude awakening when you get to Longbridge Deverill because it's only a small village but Warminster does boast two cinemas. You won't find anything at Longbridge Deverill.'

"One night I went to the pictures at the Palace in Warminster on my own. My husband was home. He hadn't gone to London then and he was still working at Bath at day, coming home at night. I used to have one night off a week and I would go to the pictures or something like that. I was watching the film and a siren went. They always used to put it up on the screen 'Siren Going'. You couldn't do anything but hear it because the siren hooter was only along the Close, not far from the Palace. There was a young soldier sat next to me. Of course you couldn't see properly in the dark but oh, he did have the fidgets. He kept on. Eventually he plucked up the courage and he looked at me and said 'Excuse me, do you ever get any air raids here?' I said 'No, you don't want to worry about that. The planes go over the top.' Well, we hadn't been sat there long when there was such a bang at the back of the seats. The doors flew open or something like that. The soldier looked at me again and he said 'Did you say no bombs dropped here?' I said 'Yes, you don't want to worry. That was a soldier fell down the stairs with his tin hat.' They had to bring their tin hats, gas masks and everything with them when they came. We all took our gas masks everywhere. We continued to watch the film. When we came out afterwards there wasn't a soul about. I thought 'This is funny, there's no one about.' I came on home, got in, and my husband was in such a paddy. I said 'What's up?' He said 'There's been an air raid.' I said 'Where?' He said 'At Corsley. They've dropped bombs! Here's me in the Red Cross and I couldn't go because you were out. Why didn't you come home?' I said 'I didn't even know there was an air raid on.' I think two soldiers were killed out there. That was when Carr's Garage, now Caffyns, was bombed. I don't think that was done on purpose. I think a German bomber was being chased by our lads and he discharged a couple of bombs he had on board. We never really got any bombs in Warminster. I think Westbury got one.

"I remember the time they bombed Bristol very badly in daylight. The planes went over here like dicky birds. I was here with my daughter Marian, and there was a lady living in the bungalow over there on her own. I thought she'd be scared out of her wits and I thought I had better go over to her. I can remember I picked up the washing-up bowl, which was enamel, and I picked up Marian in my arms. We put the washing-up bowl over our heads and ran through the hedge to stop with this old lady for company. I always remember doing that.

"We saw a lot of military activity when the Americans arrived in Warminster. We had all these huge tanks outside our house at Ash Walk. I think there were a few English ones out there too. They glided in and out and they overlapped each other for a while. The tanks out there were filthy, dirty things and they used to wash them. The road wasn't nearly as wide as it is now. A car could get up and down there but that was the only thing that really needed to because there was only the Manor House to go to. There were about six tanks at a time out here and the American ones were bigger.

"The Americans took over everything when they came. They were stationed in all different places. They were living down at Craven House and in another house on the north side of Silver Street. They were also in the Old Brewery in the High Street. Our own soldiers were in billets up the Camp at Imber Road. The Americans used to go up to the cook-house and they nicknamed it 'The Piggeries'. It was a tin hut that belonged to Lord Weymouth's Grammar School and the school used it for gymnastics. It was opposite the Bowling Green, at Ash Walk, at the back of the Grammar School. I think they nicknamed it the piggeries because there were a lot of swill bins up there and someone used to come and collect this for pigs. The Americans had so much of everything. They weren't here long, just for training. They used to walk up and down Ash Walk and they never walked in straight lines like our men did. They would march so many paces forward and then they'd walk across the road so many paces and then back again. I don't know what their idea was. The Americans we had out here were quite nice. We got on well with them and there was no trouble and no problems.

"At Christmas time they held parties for the schoolchildren of Warminster and my daughter Marian went. Of course our children didn't have very much but the Americans used to get chocolate and everything from the States. A soldier went to each house to meet the parents and it was ever such a nice young soldier that came to our house. His name was Alexander and he took Marian to the party. She never knew what it was before to have all those luxuries. The party was at the Barracks or somewhere and they took all the children to it in trucks. They had to assemble at school and the lorry picked them up. Alexander brought her back. He came in, sat down, and had a nice little chat with us. Evidently he must have asked Marian what she would like. We couldn't get dolls or anything like that. We knew nothing about this until about a month later. I can remember it as if it were only yesterday. One Sunday morning a knock came at the door and I went. It was Alexander. He had brought this lovely doll in a box, all dressed up like an American soldier, and it was a foot to two feet long. I said 'Wherever did you get that, Alexander?' He said 'Marian told me she would like a doll, she's never had a dolly, and I sent to my sister in America and she's sent it over for Marian.' She had that doll for years and we called it Alexander. She had that doll until it eventually fell to bits.

"At that time I couldn't go to church but most of the churches, including the Methodist Church at George Street, used to put on what they called 'A Social Hour' for all the soldiers. This had started when our own men were called up, before the Americans came. They would have an evening service on a Sunday night, which would be packed out, and then afterwards they would have a social hour. I couldn't go because my husband was in London but like the other women folk of the church I helped to supply them with cakes and things like that which we made from our rations. I couldn't go very often but they had a special service and our minister at that time was a chaplain to the forces and he encouraged this all he could. After the War it was really quite deadly in Warminster.

"It's quite a coincidence but one year, it must have been about 1972-74, my hubby and I went to Switzerland on our first trip abroad. We were in Interlaken, walking along, and we came across a hotel. Out there everything is covered with geraniums and flowers, and this hotel was covered with runner beans, beautiful runner beans. As we passed my husband Rowland said to me 'Goodness, it wouldn't do for those to be in Warminster, they'd get pinched!' As he said it a lady and gentleman passed us. We didn't take any notice and walked on up the road and there was a bridge across the river that joined two lakes together. When we got to the bridge the lady and gentleman were stood, leaning on it, looking over. When we got level with them the gentleman turned round and he said 'Excuse me, did I hear you mention the name of Warminster?' I said 'Yes, that's where we come from.' He said 'It was lovely to hear that. I was stationed there during the War.' I said 'Oh, were you? Well, it's a military town now.' He said 'Yes, I had some happy times there. I used to go to a canteen that was held in the Town Hall and it was run by a doctor's wife.' I said 'Yes, Doctor Hogan's wife.' He said 'Yes, and do you know, on Sunday evenings I used to go to a little chapel in a nearby street and they used to have a social hour after evening service.' I said 'You may not believe this but that's the very church we go to.' Now look, he was in Warminster during the War and this was in Interlaken we saw him in about 1972. I said to him 'Now you know where we come from, do you mind if I ask where you come from?' He said 'Grimsby.' I said 'That's quite a coincidence. A minister I knew when I was a girl, married a friend of mine from George Street, Warminster, and they were at one time posted to Grimsby.' He said 'What was his name?' I said 'The Reverend Leslie Robinson.' He said 'Oh, I know him.' It was so funny. All those miles away from home, but no matter where you go, we found, there's always someone of our generation or perhaps a little further back who knows Warminster because they've done their National Service here."

# INDEX

numbers in italics refer to illustrations

Abbeyfield 110
Acland, Chris 83
Adlam, F. *127*
Africa 81
Alcock Crest 55
Alcock, Dr 55
Alexandra, Princess 34
Alexandria 72
America 25
Americans 137
Anchor Hotel, The 128
Antigua 109 114
Argyle & Sutherland
  Highlanders 102
Arn Hill *13* 59 *59*
Artindale 12 84 86 87 88 89 93
  94 95 96 100
Artindale, Ilma 90
Artindale, Mr *84 89*
Artindale, Mrs *89 98*
Artindale, Robert Henry 96 99
Ascension Day 10 47 49
Ashburton, Lord 30
Ashman, Mrs 45
Ashton, Miss 122 123 125
Ash Walk 39 60 61 104 106
  119 *122* 127 *129* 132 137
Athenaeum, The 11 15 49 58
  70 104 128
ATS 42
Aucombe 34 *38* 114
Aucombe House 32
Australians 30 57 81

Bailey's 24
Baker, Fred 82
Baker, Rose 82
Ball, Harry 24
Ball, Percy 24
Bapton 101
Barley Close 112
Barley Research Station 75
Barracks, The 138
Barrett, Superintendent 132
Bartlett, Jimmy 45 49 51 52 53 *53*
  54 103
Bassett, W. *115*
Bassett, Walt 115 117
Bateman's 125
Bath 12 16 17 42 76 81 90 93
  95 99 120 135 136
Bath Arms, The 61
Bath, Lord 31 60
Bath, Marquis Of 31 32
Bath Road 58
Bath Wholesale Meat Company 21
Battle Abbey 102
Baverstock, B. *127*
Baverstock, Luther 12
Bazley 12
Bazley, Tom 39
Beagle Hunt Ball 118
Beaven 15
Beaven, Dr 27 112
Beckford Lodge 69 70 72 *72*
Bedminster 83
Beeches, The 49 50
Belfast 120
Belgium 20
Bellars, Rev A. R. 96
Bellew, Tom 24 47
Bell Hill 75

Bell Potteries 75
Belmont 112
Bendall, Miss 104
Bennett, Rev H. M. 84
Bexley Heath 120
Bindon, Miss 122 123 125
Bishop, Joy 135
Bishopstrow 9 76
Bishopstrow Antiques 113
Blackley, Dr 69
Blackpool 76 128
Black Watch, The 21
Bleeck's Buildings 101 106
Blind Tom 55
Bloom, Mr 40
Bloom, Mrs 40
Bloom's 40
Bloom's (Salisbury) Ltd 41
Bloom, Tom 40
Bluecaps 20
Board of Guardians, The 63
Bodnor, Corporal *48*
Boot Hill 54
Boot, The 83
Boreham 27 29 47 70 76 109
Boreham Crossroads 55
Boreham Road 9 10 17 21 23
  25 29 42 49 58 63 71 75 87
  *104 109* 109 110 112
Boughton 99
Bournemouth 21 90
Bournemouth Sea Anglers'
  Association 90
Bower, Ernest *18*
Bowling Green, The 137
Brabazon, The 121
Bradford On Avon 76 84 131
Bradley Road 26 37
Bratton 83
Brewery, The 82
Bridewell 65
Bridle, Gunner 126
Bristol 15 37 38 65 73 83 105 117 137
British Legion, The 66
Brooks, Superintendent 132
Brown 76
Brown, Bill 103
Brown, Harry 77
Bryant, Roy 101
Bryant, Miss 101
Buckenham Hall Estate 30
Buckett, Bill 117
Bugley Barton 28
Building Essentials 130
Bunch Of Grapes, The 130 131
Burgess 43 58
Burgess, Miss 106
Burton, Colonel 27
Bush & Co 24 83
Bush, Mr 44 106
Bush, Stan 106
Butcher, Geoffrey 39
Butcher, Grace 39
Butcher, Ken 6 69 70
Butcher's 69
Butcher's Bakery 87
Butcher's Yard 60
Butler, Mrs 34 110
Butler Oils 27
Butt, Molly 44 106
Button, Mr 58 131
Button's 10 131
Button's Yard 24 58

Butts Stores 43
Byways 37

Caffyns 137
Cairo 71
Calne 81 121
Cambridge 27
Cameron, Mr 115
Cameron, Nellie 34
Canada 81 102
Canadian Camp 115
Cane, W. *103*
Cannimore 47 53
Cannimore Brook, The *35*
Canon's Close 42
Cape Town 81
Carnival Old Time Dance *77*
Carr's Garage 117 137
Carson and Toone 117 121
Carson's Yard 15 17
Carter, Frank 126 127
Castle Inn *73*
Castle Laundry, The 52 106
Castle Steam Laundry *73*
Cattle Market 16
Cedars, The 45 62 *64*
Chain Lane 49 107
Chamberlain, Neville 133 134
Chambers 12 15 83
Chambers, Bert 38
Chambers, Celia *35* 38
Chambers, Miss 38
Chambers, Mr 15
Chambers, Mrs 15
Chambers, Richard 38
Chambers, Tizzie *35* 38
Channel Islands 25
Channer, Major 110
Chapel Street 106
Chapman, F. *127*
Chappell, Mr 10
Charlton 82 105
Charlton, Edgar 110
Chelmsford, Bishop Of 64
Chelwood Court 42
China 87
Chinn's 15 63
Chitterne 21
Christ Church 25 42 47 49 50
  *50* 52 54 57 70
Christ Church Football Club
  101
Christ Church Reading Room
  50
Christian, Gwendoline 125
Christian, Mr 125
Christian Science Church 106
  *129* 132
Christian Times, The 61
Christmas 12 88 95
Church Fields 105
Church Street 15 52 101 119
  132
Citadel, The 43
Citizens' Advice Bureau 81
Clapham Common 102
Clark's 21
Clevedon 15
Cley Hill 34 105 117
Clifford 57 *127*
Clifford, Matron 117
Close School, The 10 12 46 82 121 122

Close, The 58 70 104 123 125 136
Coates And Parker 75 120
Codford 9 127
Coldharbour 105
Cole's Buildings 66
Collins, Ann 22
Collins, Bill 9 *16 19 20* 22
Collins, Charles *14 16*
Collins, Charlie 9
Collins, Edna 10 *16*
Collins, Ivan *16*
Collins, Mary *14 16*
Collins, Maud *16*
Colman, Ronald 106
Congregational Church, The 123
Conservatism 65 78 89 100
Conservative Club, The 15 42
Cool, Mr 15
Co-op, The 26 66 73
Copheap 10 *13* 108 117
Copheap Lane 10 11 62 83 *107*
Corrymore 60 132
Corsley 82 117 137
Council Yard, The 104
County Hall 133
Cousins, Mr 126
Coventry 135
Cox, Marjorie 37
Cox, Ted 107
Crabtree 115
Craven House 135 137
Crayford 120
Crease, A. *14*
Crease, Archie 11 15 17 18 *18 19* 20
Crockerton 15 17 47 53 57 66 127
Crofts, Joey 84 85 87 89 96 99
Crouch, Mr 67
Crowle, Nurse *84* 84 86 87 90 93
Cruse *18* 127
Cull, Winifred 117
Cully 47
Curtis 44
Curtis, Alwyn 44
Curtis, Ann 66
Curtis, Charlie 66 67
Curtis, George 115
Curtis, Gerald 108
Curtis, H. *127*
Curtis, J. *103*
Curtis, Johnny 27
Curtis, Miss 34
Curtis, Mr 76
Curtis, Mrs 76
Curtis, Paul 109 110 114
Curtis, Roy 34 112
Cusse, Peter Samuel 26 27
Customs And Excise 120

Dairy, The 24
Dartford 120
Davies, Tom 75
Davis, Bob 72 117
Davis, Brian 83
Davis, Miss 103
Dawkins, Vic 113
Day, George 17 *19* 23
Day, Huby 39
Day, Sidney 39
Dean 15
Debenhams 42
De Gruchy *29*
De Gruchy, John 25
De Gruchy, Madam 25
Delights 12
Dene, The *79* 80
Dent's 21
Department Of The Environment 9
Deverill Road *45*
Deverills, The 15 17 47

Devizes 67 76 114
Devon 30
Devonshire 120 121
Dewey, Albert *102* 127
Dewey, Harold Nelson 10
Dewey, Mr 58 82
Dewey House 122 123
DHSS 70 80
Dickens, Charles 26
Dingles 40
Dixon, Rev 109 110 112 113 114
Dodge 117
Dodge, Mr 43
Dod Pool *116*
Doel, Mr 66 110
Donaghue, Steve 94
Doneraile Street 99
Dorset 29 54
Dorset County Council 69 72
Dossett, Mr 126
Dover House 99
Dowding 70
Dowding, Beatie 10
Dowding, Mr 53 109
Dredge, Miss 53
Dredge, Mrs 34
Drill Hall, The 70 75
Dufosee, Harry 30
Dunstan, Roy 21
Dursley 121

Eacott, Cecil 59
East End Avenue 85
East House 27 84 *85 86* 87 88
    89 90 95 96 99
Eastman 15 104
East Street *6* 10 11 12 *14* 15 16 19
    21 23 24 58 84 112
Ede, Andrew 133
Ede, Charles *121 127* 133
Ede, Godfrey 133
Ede, Marian 137
Ede, May 119 *122 136*
Ede, Rowland 133 138
Ede, Sidney 133
Edinburgh, Duke Of 31
Edmonton 120
Edwards, Mr 10
Edward, Prince 32
Edward VII 30 31 34
Egypt 71
Eldan Motors 105
Elloway 57
Elloway, A. *127*
Elloway, L. *127*
Elloway, W. *127*
Elm Hill 107
Empire Day 10
Emwell Cross House 25 *29*
Emwell Street 39 53 58 60 *124*
Evans & Allan 42
Everett, Mr 119 128
Eversfield House 127
Ex-Servicemen's Industries 62

Fair Field, The 10
Fair, The 11 12 34 70
Fairfield Road 62 70 101 126
Falk, Dr 23
Farmer's Boy, The 28
Faulkner 24
Faversham 99
Fear 47
Ferris, Mrs 119
Ferris, T. *127*
Ferris, Tom 65
Field, George 113
Field, Jack 23
Filton 121

Finch 96
First World War 81
Fish And Fruit Company 134
Fisher, Miss 42
Fisherton Delamere 87
Fitz 24
FMC 21
Foden 27
Folly Lane 54
Foreman, F. S. *103*
Foreman, Herbert 34
Foreman, Judy 34
Foreman, Mr 112
Fore Street 43 56
Fore Street Post Office 43
Foster's 16
Fowler, Mr 17
France 20
Francis, Miss 12 104
Franklin, H. *127*
Frome 9 78
Frost, Miss 44 101
Furlong, The 9 10 *11* 24 88 126

Gandy, Miss 119
Garrett 27
Gas House 58
Gateway Supermarket 127
Gay, Nelson 61 78
Gay Nineties Old Time Dance Club 76
General Strike, The 30
George, Ken 24
George Street 12 52 57 60 *73* 80
    83 104 106 115 119 123 *124*
    126 *131* 132 138
George V, King 10
Germany 20 75
Gibbs, Fred 21
Gibbs, Frederick *20* 21
Gilbert, George 59
Giles, Jack 61
Gillingham, Olive *6*
Gipsy Lane 69 *72*
Girls' British School 122 125
Girly *98*
Glasgow 115
Globe, The 57
Gloucestershire 121
Glove Factory, The 131
Glubb, Miss 39
Godolphin, J. 85
Gondoliers, The *48*
Gough's Caves *18*
Grammar School 55 101 137
Grange Park 31
Great Hall, The 34 *35*
Greening, Farmer 54
Greenland, Mr 54
Gregory 44
Grimsby 138
Grist 57
Grist, A. *127*
Grovelands Way 110
Guards 40
Guernsey 102

Haines 57
Haines, Wyndham 28
Hale, Ted 115
Halifax Building Society 119
Hall, Henry 61
Hampshire 30 31
Hampton, Bob 102 114
Hampton, Jack 114
Hampton, Roy George 101
Hampton, W. *103*
Hampton And Rowland 70
Handley, Arthur 90 95 99
Handley, Ilma 90

Handley, Ruby 90 96 99
Handley, Tommy 135
Handley, William 99
Hardiman 105
Harding, Mary 37
Harraway 39 62 *64* 108
Harraway's Nurseries *108*
Harrington, Mrs *28*
Harris 126
Harris' Mineral Water Factory 127
Harris, Mr 117
Harrods 42
Hastings 119 120
Hatchery Case 24
Hatton, Mary 39
Hatton, Mrs 39
Haversford West 20
Haygrove Farm 28
Hayward, Miss 123
Henford Marsh 53
Henley On Thames 94
Heronslade 9
Hext, Mr 75 76
Heytesbury 65
Heywood 81
Hibberd's 125
Hicks, Tommy 15
Highbury Football Club 21
Highbury House 110
High Street 15 23 72 105 107 *111* 129 134 135
Hill, Bob 66
Hill, Mark 101
Hill, Robert 82
Hillwood 37 57
Hinton, Phyllis 24
Hitler 133 135
Hockey 16
Hogan, Dr 42
Hog's Well 105
Holdoway's 133
Holland 20
Hollow, The 62
Holly Lodge 110
Holman & Byfield 24
Holmes, Mr 32 34
Holton, H. *103*
Home Guard, The 117
Horningsham *19* 21 23 69 114
Houghton, Brown, Captain 117
House, Harry 10 113
Hughes, B. *127*
Hughes, Bill 115
Hunt, Bessie 123
Huntley, Mrs C. 84

Imber 15 67 88 119 127
Imber Clump 12
Imber Downs 12
Imber Railway Bridge 128
Imber Road 10 75 101 112 137
Ingram, Bobby 76
Ingram, Daisy 62 63 64 71 *77*
Ingram, Jean 68 71 75
Ingram, Kenny 64 68 70 71 75 76
Ingram, Leonard William 43 *71 77*
Interlaken 138
International Stores 128
Ireland 65
Isle Of Wight 81
Italy 32

Jacobs, Canon 49 50
James, Mr 126
James, Phyllis 123
Jam Factory, The 62
Japan 123
Jefferies 105 106
Jennings 11

Jersey 25
Jersey Hill 115
Jersey Museum 25
Jock *40*
John, Major 65 66
John, Roland 15
John The Butcher 65
Joyce, Betty 39
Joyce, Mr 79
Joyce, Mrs 127 128

Keeping, Mr 123
Keeping, Roy 123
Kennard 94
Kent 120
Kerby, Jane 25
Kerby, Mr *26*
King 127
King Arthur, The 131
Kingdown School 70
King's Arms, The 130 131
King Street 34
Kingsway 120
Kitley, Mr W. 85
Knee, Arthur 17
KTS 127

Labour Exchange, The 65 68
Labour Government 75
Labour Party 75
Ladywell 88
Lake Pleasure Grounds *13*
Lamb, The 44
Lancashire 87
Lander, Miss 10
Langdon G. R. *103*
Langdon, Mr 54
Larkhill 114
Lawes, Mrs 10
Lawes, Mr 41
Lee, Norah *28*
Lewer, Ernie 104
Lewis, Tommy 21 24
Lewis, T. W. (Warminster) Ltd 21
Liberal Party 65
Lidbury, Florrie 37
Lister's 120
London 34 37 42 64 66 67 68 *68* 70 71 75 78 90 102 120 136
London Central Meat Company, The 16
Longbridge Deverill 34 37 53 127 135 136
Longleat *8 35* 73 115 128
Longleat Estate 26 30 31 104 112 114
Longleat House 32 34
Longleat Park *116*
Longleat Woods 29
Lord Weymouth's Grammar School 137
Low, Miss 60 62
Low, Mr 37
Lower Barn *19* 23
Lucas 101
Lucas, Austen 101 *102*
Lucas, Mr 32 101
Lucas And Foot 75
Ludgate, Miss 82 83
Ludgate, Mr 82
Ludlow Farm 26 27 28 30 37
Luxfield Road 105 106
Lymington 42 133
Lyons, Miss 10 110
Lyons, Tiger 110

Macey, Harold 117
Maiden Bradley 15
Maidenhead 71
Maidment, Bill 63
Maidment, Billy 44
Maidment, Herbie 44
Maltings, The 43

Manchester 125
Manchester Room, The 125
Manley, Mr 54
Manor Farm 37
Manor House, The 104 137
Margaret, Princess 118
Market Place 12 16 23 26 38 *46* 64 65 90 107 110 *116* 123 125 127
Marks, Sergeant *124*
Marlow, Mr 31
Marlowe, Vi 109
Marriage, Mr 9
Marsh, Bill 117
Marsh, The 10 49
Marshall, Jacob Kelk 99
Marshman's Mill 9
Mary, Princess 128
Mason, Ellen 81
Masons Arms, The 23
Maxfield, Bert 10
Meaden, Arthur Henry 81
Meaden, Ena Marjorie 99
Meaden, Fred 81 82
Meaden, Jack 81 82
Meaden, Lena 81
Meaden, Marjorie 81 *91 92 97*
Meaden, Tom 81
Mediterranean, The 71
Medlicott 110
Men's Own Brotherhood 54
Mere 32
Methodism 130
Methodist Church 104 119 125 *128* 130 *131 134* 138
Middle East, The 72
Middlesbrough 121
Midland Bank, The 125
Midlands, The 121
Miles, Eva 82
Miles, Paddy 70
Milford On Sea 133
Mills, Mr 24 57
Mills, Mrs 109
Mineral Water Factory 58
Minhinnick, Mrs 58
Minster Bible Class *102*
Minster Choir 49
Minster School 44 45 82 *124*
Minster View 110
Mole, Reg *116*
Monk, Wally 134
Montgomery 20
Montisfont Abbey Estate 30
Moody, F. *127*
Morgan Memorial Fountain 123
Mortimer, Major 104
Mortimer, R. 84
Mortimer, W. 84
Mothers' Union 76
Mud Cottages, The 127
Munday, Albert 121
Munday, Arthur 120
Munday, Elsie 120
Munday, Herbert 121
Munday, Jane 119
Munday, John 119
Munday, May 119
Mundy, Mr 24
Munich Agreement 133
Murray, Mr 21
Myrtle Avenue 126

National Health Service 72
National Service 24 138
Nelm, Mr 42
Newport (Wales) 20
News Of The World 9
Newtown School 123
New Zealand 25

Non-Conformist Cemetery, The 25
Norfolk 30
Norridge View 110
Norris, M. 84
Norris, W. 84
North Bradley 131
Northeast, Walt 17 *19* 23
Northfleet 120
North Row 10 17 26 122 123 125
Norton Bavant 15

Oaklands 110
Oak Lodge 99
Obelisk, The *2* 43 95
Obelisk Terrace 61 108
O'Donnell, Constable 51 61
Odstock Hospital 23
Old Bell Hotel, The 39 75 *77*
Oldnell, Mr 119
Ordnance Corps, The 71
Orphanage Of Pity, The 62 63 64
O'Shea, Constable 51 61
Owen, Fred 59 63
Owens 42

Palace Cinema, The *53* 58 136
Park, The 12 39 40 123
Parsonage Farm, 107
Partridge, Sergeant Major 70
Payne 104 125 126 131
Payne, Ewart 126
Payne, George 18 *18* 19
Payne, Mrs 126
Payne, William 126
Payne's Bakery 66 104
Paynton, Ron 15
Pearce, George 104
Pearce, Joyce 125
Pearce, Mr 29 43
Pearce, Percy 59
Pelly, Lady 63 110
Pembroke 20
Penn 65
Penny, Rev R. G. 34
Philipps, Sir James Erasmus 39
Picadilly Circus *68*
Pickford, Alan 25
Pickford, Austen 38
Pickford, Bernard 16
Pickford, George 39
Pickford, Hugh 38
Pickford, Mary 37
Pigot, Miss 109
Pinnell 57
Pinnell, C. *127*
Pinnell, David 119
Pinnell, Dennis 119
Pinnell, J. *103*
Pitcher, Don 113
Plants Green 42
Player, Mrs 58
Pleasures 26
Plummer & Hockey 16
Plummers 41
Plumstead Hospital 120
Police Station 106 132
Pollard, Evelyn 125
Poor Law Institution 107
Pope, John *19* 23
Poplar 64
Portsmouth 28 57
Portway 46 49 59 66 110 113
Portway House 27
Portway Railway Bridge 117
Pound Street 17 43 44 47 51 58
 59 60 61 66 76 106 112
Pound Street Recreation Ground 55 58
Pressley, E. *103*
Pressley, Jim 126

Prestbury Drive 117
Prestbury House 42 *109* 109 110 112
Prestbury Park 70
Price 57 107
Pride Of Wiltshire, The 65 114
Primrose Lane 39
Prince, Fred 105
Prince, Mr 84
Princecroft 28 30
Princecroft Lane 114 125
Prince Of Wales, The 30 31
Provo Company 20
Pullin, Mr 107

Radstock 16 26
RAF 133
Railway Station 9 17 47 58
Randall, Mr *124*
Red Cross 133 137
Red Lion, The 41
Rees, Emlyn 38
Reformatory School 54 *55* 79 83
Regal Court 12
Regency Arcade 24
Rehobath 25 30 *33* 37 *40*
Rehobath Farmhouse *32*
Reme 71 72 73 74 75
Reme Workshops *74*
Rendell 37
Reynolds, Dolly 82
Richardson *103*
Ridgeway, The 59
Robbins, Mr 23
Robin Hood Stoves 110
Robinson, Rev Leslie 138
Robinson's 20 21
Rock, Charlotte 99
Rolle, Mark 30
Roly Poly Path 85
Rose And Crown, The 24 93 117
Rotherfield Park 31
Rowe, F. *127*
Rowland 70
Royal Corps Of Military Police 20
Royal Engineers 9
Royal Square 25
Rudman, Henry 99
Rudman, Mr 84 85 96
Rule, Miss 110
Rural District Council 135
Rushton, T. J. *8*
Rutty, Jimmy 107
Ryall, Frances *28 41*
Ryall, Frances Mary 25
Ryall, Jane 25
Ryall, John *41*
Ryall, John Thomas 25 *28* 34
Ryall, Mary *28 40 41*
Ryall, Mrs *38*
Ryall, Thomas 25
Ryall's Saw Mills *31*

Sack Hill 15 67
St Bartholemew's Hospital 102
St Boniface College 50
St Denys' Convent 39 61 63 64 *67*
St John's Church 87 110 113
St John's Football Club 110
St John's Lodge 110
St John's Parish Room 110
St John's School 10 12 76
St Laurence 83
St Leonard's 102
St Monica's School *36* 39 40
St Monica's School Chapel *36*
Salisbury 20 21 40 41 42 65 125
Salisbury, Bishop Of *50*
Salisbury Plain 65
Salvation Army 43

Sambourne 58 63 *108*
Sambourne Gardens *108*
Sambourne Road 53 83 *121* 125
Sambourne School 45 52 *53* 54 57
 59 63 69 103 104 108 122
Sandhill Camp 135
Sandhill Farm 136
Sandy *40*
Sandy Hollow 49
Savernake Forest 130
Sawyer, Bob 84 *91 92* 93 95
Sawyer, Kitty 82 84 *91 92 94* 95
Sawyer, P. C. 106
Saywell, Albert 103
Scammel 27
School Of Infantry, The 21 118
Scotland 71
Scott, Fred 23
Scott, Mr 31
Scott, Mrs Robert 125
Scottish troops *46*
Scourfield, George 75
Scouts 113
Secondary School 12 57
Second World War 117 133
Service Corps, The 71
Shaftesbury 27 28
Shaftesbury Town Council 27
Sharp, Jack 126
Sharp, Mr 10 24
Sharp, Tommy 63 *102*
Shearwater *8* 29 117 127
Sheppard 16 110
Sheppard, George 17 24
Ship And Punch Bowl, The 72
Shirt And Collar Factory 47
Shoemark, Mrs 84
Silcox, Glyn 113
Silver Street 45 62 *64* 67 71 79 87
Silver Street Post Office 43
Siminson 127
Sims, John 10
Smallbrook 53 58 62 *79* 84 127
Smallbrook Farm 70 109
Smallbrook Road 107
Smith 57
Smith, Mary 25
Smith, Miss 25
Snelgrove, Ned *115*
Somerset Light Infantry 9
Southampton 42 65
Southdown House *59*
South Street 27 28
South Wraxall 84
Sparey, W. W. *103*
Spot *28*
Stalbridge Park 29
Star, The 44
Station Road 11 16 *48* 131 132
Stephens, David George 117
Stevanno 105
Stiles 24
Stiles And Gerrish 125
Stockley 41
Stockley, Frances 34
Stockley, Harry 41
Stockley, Mr 30 31 34
Stockley, Mrs Peter *28*
Stockley, Peter *28* 30 32 34
Stockley, S. 34
Stockwell 102 103
Stoke OnTrent 133
Stokes 17
Stonehenge *8*
Stourton *8*
Stuart, Rev 52 54
Sturgess, Jess 9
Style & Gerrish 42 125
Summers, Jim 105 130

Supplementary Benefit 24
Sutton Veny 15 16 17 30 47 58 67 69
Sweetland's 15
Swimming Baths 39
Switzerland 138

Talbot Villa 125
Tanswell 127
Tanswell's Garage *116* 127
Tascroft 54
Tascroft Court *55*
Taylor, Captain 82
Taylor, Charlie 63
Taylor, Fred 70 103
Taylor, Harvey 122 123
TB 70
Teddington House 53
Teichman Hall *104* 112
Temple, Squire 80
Tennis Club 40
Territorials 70 *71* 75
Tevenham, Mrs 42
Thatcher, Mrs 78
Thomas, Mr 132
Thynne, Lady Mary 128
Tidworth 70 73
Tinnams, Eddie 61
Tinnams, Ivy *22*
Tinnams, Mrs 21
Tisseman, May 25
Tisseman, Mrs 25
Titt, Cyril 62 66
Tooley *103*
Toronto Scottish Regiment 102
Torwood 25
Town Football Ground, The 9
Town Ground, The 57
Town Hall 47 58 76 80 119
Town Hall Hill 15 114 129
Town Surveyor, The 20
Trollope, Miss 10 122
Trollope, Mrs 101
Trollope, Reg 115
Trowbridge 20 46 66 78 122 123 131
Turner 57
Turner, Cecil 104 126
Turner, Mr 69 73 75
Turner And Willoughby 119
Turpin, Dick 123
Tytherington 9

Ulster Lodge 42
Upper Marsh Road 10 49
Upton House 105

Vallis, Jack 104
Verity, Mrs 83
Vicarage Street 25 *29 36* 39 43 44 46 66

Vicarage Street (continued) 82 106 108
Victoria Road 20 26 46 105 106
Vincent 57
Vincent, Mr 75
Vincent, Percy 76
Viper's Island 57

Waddington, C. *103*
Waddington, D. *103*
Waddington, David 63
Wake, Rev H. 96 113
Wales 20 57 81
Wall, Mabel 120
Walters, Miss 104
Walthamstow 120
Ward, Albany 58
Wardour Castle *8*
Warminster Bookshop 15
Warminster Common 15 18 23 26 27 37
Warminster Conservative Club 95
Warminster Downs 117
Warminster Fire Brigade *102* 112 127
Warminster Flying Club 87
Warminster History Society 23
Warminster Hospital 23 *113* 113 117
Warminster Journal, The 80
Warminster Motor company 60
Warminster Operatic Society *46* 49 126
Warminster Post Office 54
Warminster Registry Office 125
Warminster Reserves Football Club 57
Warminster Rubbish Dump 12
Warminster School 39
Warminster Timber Company 54 62 64
   65 101 110 114 *115 116* 128
Warminster Town Band 43 95
Warminster Town Council *8* 27
Warminster Town Football
   Club 57 101 *103*
Warminster Town Football Ground 54
Water Board, The 128
Waterloo 81
Waters, C. *127*
Waylen, Captain 117
Waylen, Vera 135
Webb, S. *111*
Webb, Sammy 104
Webber, Dick 72
Webster, Mr 95
Weights And Measures 20
Welling 120
Wellworthy's 42 133
Wesley Guild 130
Wesley Road 131
Westbury 20 73 78 81
Westbury Iron Works 81
Westbury Road *59*
Westbury Station 37

Westbury White Horse *8*
West End 64
Weston, Mr 44
Weston Super Mare Cricket Club 17
West Parade 47 54 55 60 126 *127* 133
West Street 59 62 64 66 69 82
   101 103 104 105 106
Weymouth *71* 81 99 119 130
Weymouth Arms, The *124*
Weymouth Street 9 11 *13* 39 54
   58 68 70 105 *121* 133
Wheeler's Imperial Cabbage *112* 114
Wheeler's Nurseries 69 112
Whistler, Capt. A. J. 90
Whistler Major 15
Whitbread 15
White, Jimmy 24 93
White Hart, The 104 123 135
Whitmarsh, Edgar 24
Whitmarsh, Frank 23 125
Whitmarsh, J. L. *103*
Whitmarsh, Mrs Frank 125
Whittle, George 117
Willcox, Claude *56* 60 61 62 *124*
Willcox, Hubert 37
Willoughby, Mr 130 131
Willoughby, Mrs 130
Wills, Percy 117
Wilson & Kennard 42 90
Wilson Square *74*
Wiltshire Agricultural Show 9
Wiltshire County Council *107*
Wiltshire County Council Egg
   Laying Trials 108
Wimbledon 40 133
Wincanton Races 41
Windsor 70
Withers, John 21
Withey, B. *127*
Withey, Benny 130 *131*
Woodcock 70 110
Woodcock House 65
Woodrow, James 30
Workhouse, The 24 26 47 54
Worthington 104
Wrens, The 120
Wright, Bernie 88
Wright, George 61 76
Wright, Mr 88
Wyatt, Bunny 67 68 69
Wyatt, Mrs 68
Wylye 88
Wylye, River 62 *79*
Wylye Valley 127

Yeates, Harold 83 100
Yeates, Marjorie 81
Yeovil 120

---

# DO YOU REMEMBER?

The original tape recordings of the interviews featured in this book, plus others, are deposited at Warminster Dewey Museum. Danny Howell is keen to add to the Museum's oral history archive relating to Warminster and the surrounding villages. If you are aged 60 or over and are willing to have your reminiscences recorded in this way, Danny would be delighted to hear from you. He may be contacted at Warminster Dewey Museum, Three Horseshoes Mall, Warminster.

# OTHER BOOKS BY DANNY HOWELL

**Scratchbury Hill And Other Poems**
(self-published)
December 1983

**An Old Postcard Album Of Warminster**
(published by the Wylye Valley Life)
November 1985

**Yesterday's Warminster**
(published by Barracuda Books)
April 1987

**The Wiltshire Foundry, Warminster, 1816-1909**
(published by Wylye Valley Publications)
November 1987

**Smallbrook Farm, Warminster, 1905-1965**
(published by Wylye Valley Publications)
April 1988

**Warminster, The Way We Were**
(published by Wylye Valley Publications)
November 1988

**The Wylye Valley In Old Photographs**
(published by Alan Sutton Publishing)
November 1988

**Three Recommended Walks From Bishopstrow House Hotel**
(published by Bishopstrow House Hotel)
May 1989

**Warminster In Old Photographs**
(published by Alan Sutton Publishing)
November 1989

**Remember The Wylye Valley**
(published by Danny Howell)
November 1989

**Five Connected Lives**
(published by Danny Howell Books)
May 1990